The Scarlet Thread

Tainted Women

SHERNETT ROSE FORD

WESTBOW
PRESS®
A DIVISION OF THOMAS NELSON
& ZONDERVAN

Scripture taken from the New King James Version®. Copyright © 1982 by Thomas Nelson. Used by permission. All rights reserved.

Scripture quotations marked (KJV) taken from the King James Version.

Scripture quotations taken from the Amplified® Bible (AMP), Copyright © 2015 by The Lockman Foundation Used by permission. www.Lockman.org

Scriptures taken from the Holy Bible, New International Version®, NIV®. Copyright © 1973, 1978, 1984, 2011 by Biblica, Inc.™ Used by permission of Zondervan. All rights reserved worldwide. www.zondervan.com The "NIV" and "New International Version" are trademarks registered in the United States Patent and Trademark Office by Biblica, Inc.™

Scripture quotations taken from the New American Standard Bible® (NASB), Copyright © 1960, 1962, 1963, 1968, 1971, 1972, 1973, 1975, 1977, 1995 by The Lockman Foundation Used by permission. www.Lockman.org

WestBow Press books may be ordered through booksellers or by contacting:

WestBow Press
A Division of Thomas Nelson & Zondervan
1663 Liberty Drive
Bloomington, IN 47403
www.westbowpress.com
1 (866) 928-1240

Because of the dynamic nature of the Internet, any web addresses or links contained in this book may have changed since publication and may no longer be valid. The views expressed in this work are solely those of the author and do not necessarily reflect the views of the publisher, and the publisher hereby disclaims any responsibility for them.

Any people depicted in stock imagery provided by Thinkstock are models, and such images are being used for illustrative purposes only. Certain stock imagery © Thinkstock.

ISBN: 978-1-5127-6188-7 (sc)
ISBN: 978-1-5127-6190-0 (hc)
ISBN: 978-1-5127-6189-4 (e)

Library of Congress Control Number: 2016917957

Print information available on the last page.

WestBow Press rev. date: 11/11/2016

This book reviews the lives of women who were involved in Christ's ancestry. It examines their flaws and weaknesses, how they triumphed over them, and how they were used by God to carry out his work on earth.

Contents

Introduction

Then God said, "Let Us make man in Our image, according to Our likeness; let them have dominion over the fish of the sea, over the birds of the air, and over the cattle, over all the earth and over every creeping thing that creeps on the earth." So God created man in His own image; in the image of God He created him; male and female He created them. Then God blessed them, and God said to them, "Be fruitful and multiply; fill the earth and subdue it; have dominion over the fish of the sea, over the birds of the air, and over every living thing that moves on the earth." (Genesis 1:26–28 NKJV)

God created the most awesome place outside of heaven and after affirming that it was good, He decided to share it with a creature that would be made in his "image and likeness." He lovingly made man from the dust of the earth and then made a beautiful mate, comparable to him, to be his companion. He did not leave them helpless but gave them the ability to reproduce and have dominion over every created thing on the earth. Man had divine authority to use the earth and its substance for sustenance and pleasure without limitations, except the tree of the knowledge of good and evil. God clearly told Adam in Genesis 2:15–17 that he was restricted from eating from this tree, and also the consequences for disobeying his command.

Then the Lord God took the man and put him in the Garden of Eden to tend and keep it. And the Lord God commanded the man, saying, "Of every tree of the garden you may freely eat; but of the tree of the knowledge of good and evil you shall not eat, for in the day that you eat of it you shall surely die."(Gen. 2:15–17 NKJV).

Had not God been more than generous in limiting access to only one tree to Adam and his wife from his total creation? Adam was to be the keeper of the garden so it would remain in the pristine form with which God had created it, and perhaps to prevent any alien creature from entering it. That is what God expected from Adam, and not Eve, because responsibility goes with authority. Having been warned and vested with divine backing, it would be hard, if not impossible, for any creature apart from the Creator to convince Adam to eat of the restricted tree. Thus, Satan, knowing what he was up against in prompting Adam to disobey God's warning, used Adam's own flesh to undermine him—that is, someone who had legal access to him. That person was Eve. The crafty devil perhaps heard Adam declare Eve as "bone of my bone and flesh of my flesh" (Gen. 2:23) and thought that Adam's desire would be to please his wife. If she offered him an apple, her action would appear quite harmless and not directly subversive to her husband's authority. Apparently, Eve had previously looked at the tree with longing, so Satan appealed to her desire for the fruit and ultimately she was "drawn away by her own lust." She yielded to temptation without considering that her action was open defiance of the authority with which God had entrusted Adam, and even worse—disregard for the immutable word of the Creator of the universe!

Whenever we cross the line that God draws outside of our sphere of authority, we become dull of hearing and unable to see clearly. How did Eve go outside God's line? By having her mind set on the forbidden object and not on the bountifulness of all the other things God had richly given her to use as she wished. Outside of God's line of vision, she had a distorted view of what was around her; therefore, she had a decreased sense of God and a heightened awareness of the fruit. She may have been oblivious to the movement of the serpent as he stealthily slithered on the floor of the garden, but she immediately responded to the question that he posed: "Has God indeed said, 'You shall not eat of every tree of the garden?'" Without any hesitation she rattled off God's command to the serpent like meaningless rote because she had a greater desire for the fruit than for the word of God.

It was not the first time that Eve had seen the fruit, but this time her eyes bewitched her. They bewitched her because her heart was not in the right place. Satan did not have to do much to convince Eve to eat the fruit. All he had to do was to ask the leading question, wait, and then make a follow-up statement. He watched as Eve lusted after the fruit, swooped it from the tree, brought it to her mouth, and sank her teeth into it. Up to this point, the serpent's plan had succeeded without a hitch; however, he was not ready to gloat until Adam had eaten the fruit. It was not difficult because Eve had already picked a fruit for her husband. Adam took the fruit without hesitation and ate it without questioning his wife, knowing such an action was outward rebellion against God.

> So when the woman saw that the tree was good for food, that it was pleasant to the eyes, and a tree desirable to make one wise, she took of its fruit and ate. She also gave to her husband with her, and he ate. Then the eyes of both of them were opened, and they knew that they were naked; and they sewed fig leaves together and made themselves coverings. (Gen. 3:6–7 NKJV)

Adam realized too late what he had done. He underestimated the subtlety of the devil and took his eyes off the Creator. It is therefore clear that in order for Adam's power to work at its optimum level, it had to remain connected to its source in the same way that an electrical cord always has to be plugged into a socket to transfer energy to an object. The flow of electrical energy will invariably stop in an unplugged cord regardless of how long it remains away from its source because the latter is the repository and the plug remains ineffective without its continuous replenishment. Similarly, authority is vested in a person by one who has greater power. Extensive liberty may be given to the holder; however, such liberty has boundaries. If the holder has unbridled power, he is accountable to no one and could ultimately hurt himself and others. God established a chain of authority on earth: Adam was the head of his wife, her covering and protector; God was his covering and protector and the ultimate head of all creation. Eve, who was created to be Adam's helpmate, would share all the rights and privileges that her husband enjoyed if she obeyed God's directives. She was expected to subject herself to Adam's authority as he too honored God's authority.

However, Adam relinquished his authority to his wife by clearly sanctioning her act of disobedience by eating the fruit that she offered him. He had means, motive, and opportunity to expel the devil from the garden before the act of sin was committed. He had the means of authority and choice; his motive was God told him that the day he ate of the forbidden fruit he would surely die, and the opportunity was that he had enough time to remind his wife of God's command, to seek God's help, and to rebuke the serpent. The Bible states that Adam was with Eve when she ate the fruit because "she took some and ate it. She also gave some to her husband, who was with her, and he ate it" (Gen. 3:6).

That means that Adam was not in another part of the garden when the serpent slipped in without his knowledge and deceived his wife. He watched and listened passively as the devil beguiled the woman that God had committed to Adam's care. The serpent was not unknown to him because God had brought all creatures to him and given him the honor to name all of them as he pleased (Gen. 2:19–20). Apparently, he knew the natural characteristic of the serpent, and that is why he named him thus. If Adam was not aware of its nature and its portentous presence, there is reasonable doubt that the Bible would have emphasized in the beginning of Genesis 3:1 that:

> Now the serpent was more crafty than any of the wild animals the Lord God had made. He said to the woman, "Did God really say, 'You must not eat from any tree in the garden?'"

Another note of interest is the fact that it was Adam, not God, who called the creature made from his rib *woman* after God presented her to him. After their commission of disobedience, he named her *Eve* to signify that she would be the mother of all subsequent generations on earth (Gen. 3:20). That God would allow a mere mortal to name the objects of His creation, including his wife, is inconceivable, but God did so that man's authority would be without question. Therefore, Adam was without excuse for not resisting the serpent. God could have intervened during the time of the temptation, but God had given man free choice and expected Adam to exercise the authority given to him. After all, God had been very clear in His instructions to Adam and given him the authority to subdue not some, but all creatures on earth, under the waters, and in the air.

Apparently, Adam thought lightly of his obligation to his wife, his antecedents, and God, so he allowed the serpent to have free reign in the territory with which he was entrusted. Like Esau, who would be born centuries after him, he surrendered his "inheritance" for instant gratification: his for a fruit and Esau's for a pottage of stew. Although not sharing the same type of responsibility as her husband, Eve did not escape God's consequences of her action. She had let the lust for the forbidden fruit cloud her wisdom. Instant gratification gave way to an eternal consequence for her and all her descendants. By sinning, she inadvertently allowed what was already decreed to come into effect through Jesus Christ. Eve was therefore the unwary catalyst both in the downfall and redemption of humankind.

God declared enmity between Eve and the serpent and not her husband because she would be the mother of all living persons. Although Adam carried the seed for all humanity, Eve would produce the children that would originate from him. Moreover, Jesus would be the seed that would be borne by *woman* (Mary**),** begotten of God, and not engendered by *man*. Jesus would ultimately "crush the head of the serpent" and the latter would "strike his heel" (Gen. 3:15 NKJV):

> I will put enmity
> between you and the woman,
> and between your offspring and hers;
> he will crush your head,
> and you will strike his heel.

God has fitted all of humanity with a free will, and He allows us to exercise it with the freedom of choice. Note that the damage the serpent would do to Eve is minimal compared to what she and her offspring would do to him. A strike to the head often renders one unconscious, but the crushing of one's head results in the death of the victim. Satan temporarily "bruised the heel" of the woman's seed while Christ experienced betrayal and death, but Christ's victory through resurrection and ascension "crushed the head" of the devil. God knew before the foundation of the world that humans would fall and it would take the intervention of the sinless Lamb to bring them back to their rightful place with Him. The question that arises is: If God knew that Adam and Eve would commit a sin that would negatively impact the whole human race, why didn't He prevent it?

There is really no neat answer to this question, and to try to give one that may sound reasonable in defense of God is a weak attempt to pander to human sensibility. Our motives may be pure because we want to protect the name of the Almighty Creator; nevertheless, we must be reminded that there are some things that will remain inexplicable unless God reveals them to us. It may be a hard pill to swallow, but God does reserve the right to reveal what He wills to His creation. God is sovereign and His ways are higher than our ways; His judgments are unsearchable and his ways are past finding out (Rom. 11:33). One of the greatest anomalies of the Bible is that Jesus chose twelve disciples and one of them betrayed Him. The omniscient, omnipotent God of heaven and earth deliberately chose a man to be His disciple whom He knew beforehand would undermine Him. However, we also know that the act of betrayal by Judas Iscariot that was designed to destroy Jesus's ministry worked in the plan of God's redemption and reconciliation for humankind.

Our job as created beings is not to question the actions of the Creator but to accept that God knows what He is doing. What if God wants to display His mighty powers in the lives of those whom He loves? "For God so loved the world, that he gave his only begotten Son, that whosoever believeth in him should not perish but have everlasting life" (John 3:16). The truth is that God gave Adam and Eve a command and they disobeyed. Eve was not tempted in any way by God to succumb to the wiles of Satan, since Jesus clearly states in the New Testament that a house divided against itself cannot stand (Mark 3:32). Simply put, God never tempts His children and cannot be tempted by them. He was utterly displeased when Eve sinned against Him because He knew that her action would cause separation from Him and a downward spiritual spiral of every generation into degradation.

Nevertheless, God provided a way of escape for her and all those who would originate from her and Adam. He gave them a foreshadowing of the all-encompassing grace that would culminate in Christ's victory on the cross when He performed the first blood sacrifice in the garden of Eden. God made covering from the skins of animal for Adam and Eve when they found out that they were naked and were ashamed of their state (Gen. 3:21). In so doing, God provided a token of redemption for their sin with the blood of animals. As we already know, the shedding of animal blood served only as a temporary fix because a perfect blood price had to be paid to completely cover Adam's sin and reconcile him and his seed back to his relationship with God since sin was imputed to us through Adam and not through Eve.

CHAPTER 1

The Virgin

How Can This Be?

Time is priceless—it can be neither bought nor sold. It encapsulates everything that is done or not done under the sun, and no mortal transcends it. Therefore, the Creator took His time and meticulously fashioned woman from man's rib as an indication of the value He placed on her. He also chose one virgin girl to become the mother of His Son before Adam and Eve even conceived their first child. Like God did with Adam, He could have allowed Jesus to come to earth as a grown man. However, He bypassed human expectation and prepared the womb of a virgin girl to receive Him. The honor was conferred on Mary.

Mary was young and unsophisticated, yet she was wise in the things of God. She was engaged to be married to a humble carpenter named Joseph. He was a devout adherent of Jewish law and a just man (Matt. 1:19), as one would have expected the earthly father of God's only begotten Son to be. He was a loyal friend of her family and trusted that the young girl who would be his bride would be faithful to him. Little did he know that his chaste virgin would be carrying a child who was not fathered by him or by any man on earth! Despite his shock and disappointment—and being older and wiser than she was—something in him wanted to protect this young girl, so he planned to put her away privately.

So he had had many sleepless nights since she told him about her encounter with an angel—and even more preposterously that she was impregnated through the power of the Holy Spirit! How could this be possible since she claimed she was still a virgin? Yet her eyes only showed sincerity when he looked at her. Where did she get that calm, knowing that she could be stoned to death for her apparent infidelity? His life was simple until he became betrothed to this beautiful young girl.

Mary too led a simple life until the day the angel appeared to her and told her that she was highly favored and blessed among women. Up to this point in her life, except perhaps for the annual pilgrimage to Jerusalem for the Passover and sometimes other Jewish feasts, her betrothal to Joseph may have been the most eventful. She was no stranger to the Mosaic law and knew that when she accepted betrothal, she was entering into an agreement that was as binding as marriage. Although she was young, she understood its seriousness and the severe consequences that she would receive if she dishonored this sacred rite.

It was enough to tell her that she was special among women, but that she would be the mother of the Messiah was inconceivable to her, regardless of the belief that it was every Jewish girl's dream. However, no one expected that the girl would be from a humble background in an insignificant place in Israel. Moreover, the miraculous conception of a human without the combination of a sperm and an egg was unheard of—and not even thought of in the minds of many Jewish people. Notwithstanding, the prophet Isaiah had foretold it centuries before its occurrence:

> "Behold, a virgin shall be with child, and shall bring forth a son, and they shall call his name Emmanuel, which being interpreted is, God with us" (Matt 1:23 NKJV).

Mary asked the angel the same question that probably ran through Joseph's mind: "How can this thing be seeing I know not a man? (Luke 1:34 KJV). What must be understood in Mary's response to the angel is that she did not express doubt about God's ability to fulfill His word; rather she asked how it would occur since she had never slept with a man. Her reaction to Gabriel was in contrast to the husband of her cousin, who also received news earlier from the angel that his wife, Elizabeth, was going to bear a son after being barren all her life. The Gospel of Luke gives an account of the birth of Christ's forerunner, John the Baptist. It tells how his father, Zacharias, became dumb because he did not believe the angel's word that God would bless him and his wife to produce a child in their old age. Zacharias was a priest and was expected to have knowledge of the scriptures; therefore, his question to the angel was unacceptable:

> And Zacharias said to the angel, "How shall I know this? For I am an old man, and my wife is well advanced in years." And the angel answered and said to him, "I am Gabriel, who stands in the presence of God, and was sent to speak to you and bring you these glad tidings. But behold, you will be mute and not able to speak until the day these things take place, because you did not believe my words which will be fulfilled in their own time." (Luke 1:18–20 NKJV)

Mary's response to the news of her impending pregnancy elicits further explanation from Gabriel and not reproof because it was expressed out of curiosity rather than the skepticism shown by Zacharias. Unlike Zacharias, who could find records in the Old Testament of barren women like Sarah who bore children in their old age, Mary had no precedent for conception without the intervention of a man and woman. She gladly accepted God's design for her life after the angel explained that the Holy Ghost would come upon her and then she would conceive. Not only had the Holy Ghost caused her to conceive a living embryo in her womb but He also filled her with complete peace. Her words to the angel reveal her simple faith in Yahweh: "'I am the Lord's servant … may your word to me be fulfilled.' Then the angel left her" (Luke 1:38 NKJV).

Even if she had been anxious about Joseph's reaction to her pregnancy, surprisingly, this young girl did not doubt that the angel's words about her being the mother of the Savior of the world were true; she was only perplexed by the manner in which it would occur. She asked the most logical question, knowing that babies were produced through sexual relations between a man and a woman and that it was not yet time for Joseph and her to cohabitate. The consummation of Jewish marriages in Mary's day usually took place after the betrothal. The child was to be the Son of God, pure and holy, yet He would be conceived by a mother who had to go to the temple and ask a priest to offer sacrifices for her sins!

Mary was a girl who was subject to the passions of any teenage girl of her era who had grown up in the Jewish faith. She understood the law because, like any other Jewish girl, she had been taught the scriptures and was familiar with the teachings on sexual immorality. Perhaps she had seen firsthand or heard of the fate of girls who were accused of committing adultery, and perhaps she cringed to think that she could also be stoned if she was found to be pregnant before her marriage was consummated with Joseph. Not only would she be disgraced, but her family would be disgraced as well. And Joseph? Even if he was found to be innocent of her "sin," it would have been embarrassing and painful for him because of his love and respect for her. Though young, Mary may have pondered these things in her heart. However, she made the decision to submit her will to God and trusted Him to clean up the mess. What great faith and humility!

God's heart was tender toward her, knowing that she was but a girl—and one who had lived a sheltered life. Jesus, who had lived in the warmth of her womb for nine months and had been nourished by her placenta, was also privy to the innermost fibrillations of her heart. As Mary pondered the wonders of the life growing within her and thought about her divine experiences, the developing fetus simultaneously translated her unsaid utterances by the power of the Holy Spirit. Strange as it may sound to us, it was not improbable in the realms of God's kingdom. If John, Jesus's forerunner, leaped for joy in the womb of his mother at the sound of Mary's greeting, how much more would the Son of God be attuned to the musings of his mortal mother? His unique position as both Son of God and Son of man allowed Him to understand the heart of the so-called weaker sex; therefore, it is no wonder that women served a special role in His ministry.

Mary had developed a special bond with her eldest son as He grew into a man. Her husband, who was older than she was, had died when she was in the prime of her life—and Jesus would have most likely taken on the responsibility of taking care of His mother. He had learned carpentry from Joseph and was expected to use His skills to support the family in His father's absence.

For a number of years, Jesus seemed to disappear after He went into the temple at the age of twelve and confounded the priestly elite with His unprecedented wisdom. He shocked His parents and was apparently unconcerned that they had sought Him for three days while He remained in Jerusalem calmly explaining to adults and answering questions relating to the scriptures. If Mary felt any pride that her twelve-year-old was outwitting learned men, such admiration was overshadowed by her anger at His seeming indifference. Like any anxious mother, she chided Him:

> His parents went to Jerusalem every year at the Feast of the Passover. And when He was twelve years old, they went up to Jerusalem according to the custom of the feast. When they had finished the days, as they returned, the Boy Jesus lingered behind in Jerusalem. And Joseph and His mother did not know it; but supposing Him to have been in the

company, they went a day's journey, and sought Him among their relatives and acquaintances. So when they did not find Him, they returned to Jerusalem, seeking Him. Now so it was that after three days they found Him in the temple, sitting in the midst of the teachers, both listening to them and asking them questions. And all who heard Him were astonished at His understanding and answers. So when they saw Him, they were amazed; and His mother said to Him, "Son, why have You done this to us? Look, Your father and I have sought You anxiously."

And He said to them, "Why did you seek Me? Did you not know that I must be about my Father's business?" But they did not understand the statement which He spoke to them. (Luke 1:41–50 NKJV)

The Bible notes that after Jesus revealed His purpose for lingering in the temple, He subjected His will to the authority of His parents. Nevertheless, His mother "kept all these things in her heart" (Luke 2–51) because what was happening could not be shared with the people around her. They could only be understood by divine revelation. Jesus, Creator of all things, felt the heartbeat of His mother, and knew her concerns firsthand. There is no question that she was filled with the Holy Spirit from the time of the conception of Jesus and while she carried the living Word in her womb. Her pregnant cousin Elizabeth became instantaneously filled with the Holy Ghost and confessed that as soon as the voice of Mary's greeting sounded in her ears, her baby "leaped in her womb for joy" (Luke 1:44).

Mary had the opportunity to meditate on the phenomenal events that were taking place in her life and to receive illumination from the resident Holy Spirit within her. If we who have the Holy Spirit living in us have access to his revelation and teaching, how much more the mother of Jesus received His wisdom as she bore God's holy Son. He was not without power, although He was wrapped in human flesh, because the Holy Spirit guided Him. Without the revelation and the empowerment of the Holy Ghost, Mary could not have submitted to bearing a child amid the whispers and perhaps even taunts of people who thought that Joseph had lost his mind.

Even his closest and most loyal friends and relatives must have been baffled by Joseph's loyalty to her despite the shame she had brought to him. She had made him a laughingstock as if she were completely unaware of the consequences for flouting sacred Jewish laws and marriage customs.

However, all his life Joseph had heard all the incredible things that Yahweh had done in the life of his people, and he too had read and believed the scriptures. His inclination to please God outweighed his desire to put away Mary although he had a justifiable reason to do so. Our postmodern courts perhaps would have annulled his betrothal based on irreconcilable differences, and Mary would have been accepted as a single mother.

In God's order, this was not going to work!

Jesus Christ would be brought into the world under the legal covering of a father because God never contradicts Himself. Joseph was the one chosen from King David's line to assume that role. When the angel of the Lord appeared to him in a dream and assured him that the child Mary had conceived was of the Holy Ghost and he should not be afraid to marry her, Joseph believed and immediately acted (Matt. 1:19–25). He took Mary as his wife and by his obedience aborted the swirling rumors about her chastity and perhaps even her death. Hadn't God said in His word to Moses that He would have mercy on whom He will? (Rom. 9:15). He had blessed not only Mary to be the mother of the Messiah but also Joseph to be His earthly father. Jesus would be born to poor but godly parents.

His transition from heaven to earth was prepared for Him, though not in the way the Jews had envisioned that the Son of God would be born. He would not have all the trappings of wealth as they expected. Like all humankind who came from Adam, He would develop naturally in the womb of a female. He came in contact with blood and water inside the uterus of Mary since He received nourishment from His mother's placenta and was born as a result of natural labor:

> Since the children have flesh and blood, He Himself likewise also partook of the same that through death He might render powerless him who had the power of death, that is, the devil, and might free those who through fear of death were subject to slavery all their lives. (Hebrews 2:14–15 NKJV)

After Adam and Eve committed sin in the garden of Eden, the preincarnate Christ participated in an act of blood sacrifice in which He used skins as a covering for both man and woman. The Bible does not directly state that animals were killed, but it is obvious that since both Adam and Eve used leaves to cover their bodies, there were no skins available. Therefore animals had to be killed, and that was not done by the guilty Adam and his wife, but by God. The spilling of animal blood here is a precursor of what was to come in the New Testament through Jesus Christ, who is the spotless Lamb of God.

At Jesus's death, blood and water gushed out as the Roman soldier pierced His side. The uterus of Mary was also a safe haven, in which the Savior was protected by amniotic fluid. Water is one of the most common and precious elements on earth. The Son of man, unlike Adam, experienced it as His shelter because he would be the one who would cleanse us from our sins:

> This is the one who came by water and blood—Jesus Christ. He did not come by water only, but by water and blood. And

it is the Spirit who testifies, because the Spirit is the truth (1 John 5:6 NKJV).

Therefore, Jesus was the "firstborn over all creation" (Col. 1:15 NKJV) and not Adam because the latter was created as an adult by the hand of Christ and His Father, God Almighty. Nevertheless, Adam was given authority over all living things, though not the same authority as Christ, "[who is] before all things, and in Him all things consist" (Col. 1:17 NKJV). Adam was created, but Christ was begotten; thus, He had the power to appoint the time when He would take on a body, lay down his life, and be resurrected.

Mary was the only woman, and will be the only woman, on earth who has had the great honor of being the mother of our Savior. She was highly favored before the foundations of the earth were laid because God looked through the telescope of time and knew that she would willingly submit to His will. Had she resisted, no one knows what would have been the fate of humankind.

CHAPTER 2

Eve

The Apple of My Eye

Eve is the mother of all mothers. She was the first woman, lovingly created by God, and bore the original imprint of the Creator Himself. It is not that we all do not have the stamp of God in our bodies, but Adam and Eve were hewn and fashioned by the hand of God. They literally felt His touch and the living breath of God as it filled the chambers of their bodies. Unlike other humans born after them, they had not experienced the warmth of a mother's womb or the progression of life from infancy to adulthood. Adam and Eve were created as adults.

God created Adam and placed the stamp in him that would be carried from generation to generation. He stocked his loins with the seminal blueprint for the perpetuation of humanity. God, already knowing that it was not good for man to be alone, gave him a companion. He caused Adam to fall into a deep sleep and carefully took a rib from him and wrought the most ingenious workmanship that was befitting of what David would later exclaim about himself, "I will praise thee; for I am fearfully and wonderfully made: marvellous are thy works; and that my soul knoweth right well" (Ps. 139:14). When Adam woke from his slumber and set eyes on the most resplendent terrestrial being he had ever seen, he gushed, "This is bone of my bones, flesh of my flesh: she shall be called 'Woman' because she was taken out of 'Man'"

(Gen. 2:23 NKJV). He would cleave to his wife, forsaking all others and leaving mother and father to fulfill the laws of procreation. The woman would submit to him, as she trusted in his protection. Eve had no need to fear; her only "dis-ease" was that nagging feeling she sometimes had from looking at that beautiful fruit she was prohibited from eating in the midst of the garden. God had placed a hedge of protection around her as she walked within the authority of her husband, Adam.

The Creator had also given her the ability to exercise free will. However, Eve mistook free will for "have it your way." In God's kingdom, free will means you have special privileges and rights, access to all His blessings, and protection if you subject yourself to His guidance. Jesus said that His yoke was easy and His burdens were light. Eve mistakenly saw the "yoke" of avoiding the tree of the knowledge of good and evil cumbersome until she realized the heavy yoke of the consequences of sin. After she rebelled against God's orders in the garden of Eden, God told her that she would bring forth a child in pain. God also told her that the serpent would bruise her heel and she would bruise his head.

On hearing God's words, neither Adam nor Eve understood the ramifications of those utterances. They knew that they would be expelled from the garden, but they did not know that even in punishment God had provided a way of escape for those "whose breath is in [their] nostrils" (Isa. 2:22 NKJV). No devil in hell would gain complete control of the earth that Jehovah had lovingly made for Himself and those who wore His likeness and carried His stamp. The wheels of eternity had started turning as God declared part of the fate of Satan. Time took greater notice from that moment to prepare Immanuel's entrance into earth's sphere and save all humanity from the throes of the enemy. Eve had unwittingly changed the course of history. She did not know that from her loins would come the seed that would continue through generations to bring forth Mary, who would bear the Son of God to undo the nefarious web of her error.

"O the depth of the riches both of the wisdom and knowledge of God! How unsearchable are his judgments and his ways are past finding out!" (Rom. 11:33 NKJV*).*

The word of God never returns to Him void; in other words, His word is never wasted. The word of God flows through His breath, and from that breath He gave life to man. He breathed into man and he became a "living soul." Why then would God allow His creation into whom He had breathed His precious breath and placed His stamp to be left on earth to languish without redemption? Our God is not slothful in business. He is thorough in all His ways.

God did not allow the body of Jesus Christ to stink or rot in the grave to show that death only came about because of sin. Jesus died, but He remained in the grave only three days, and then He was resurrected. Be aware that God could have resurrected His Son had He been stinking in the grave, and we have proof from the Bible that Jesus raised Lazarus when his body had started to decompose. However, it was not to be the fate of the sinless Lamb. Of course born-again Christians die a natural death, but they will rise again. Since humans have been touched by sin, they will go to the grave, but they cannot remain there forever if they have been changed by the blood of Christ. Those who face eternal death are those whose lives have not been transformed by the blood of Jesus. The Bible states in I Corinthians 15:55, "O death where is thy sting? O grave where is thy victory?"

Although Satan thought that he had irked God by outwitting Adam through the naiveté of his wife, such guile only complicated the web in which Lucifer had entangled himself. In his arrogance, he failed to foresee that vaunting himself against God would precipitate his ejection from heaven. How many times had God used the foolish things of the world to confound the wise? Of course Eve had been foolish and disobedient. Through her action she had caused Adam to give up his dominion over the things of the earth. Yet God had a plan that would redeem His most prized creation and would come from the womb of a woman. Sin entered the world through the compliance of one woman and the execution of one man, and it was destroyed by the obedience of one woman and the total commitment of one man.

God used the so-called weaker sex to "bruise the head of the serpent" just as He had declared in the garden of Eden. Jesus Christ, who would be our Redeemer, was fully God and fully man. He came through the loins of a woman who was untouched by the embrace of a man. The Holy Ghost overpowered her, and she conceived Immanuel (God with us). Like the first Adam, Christ's existence had not come through coitus between man and woman; however, He developed normally as any other human being in the womb of a woman. Moreover, though begotten of God, the pregnancy of His virgin mother was validated by her marriage to His earthly father, Joseph. No one could challenge His right to die for humanity and take back its dominion on the earth. Not even the devil.

Unlike Adam, Christ was not placed on the earth as a fully grown adult. He was the legitimate seed of Abraham, whom God had chosen to be the father of many nations and to whom He declared that from His seed all nations would be blessed.

> And [God] said: "By Myself I have sworn, says the Lord, because you have done this thing, and have not withheld your son, your only *son*—blessing I will bless you, and multiplying I will multiply your descendants as the stars of the heaven and as the sand which *is* on the seashore; and your descendants shall possess the gate of their enemies. In your seed all the nations of the earth shall be blessed, because you have obeyed My voice." (Gen. 22:16–18 NKJV)

God had given Adam total dominion over the earth and all things in it. Through sin Adam had relinquished his authority, but God had made it possible that through Abraham it would be restored in the earth through a man who was not a product of human cohabitation. We know from scripture that even those who are not born of natural Jewish lineage are also heirs of Abraham's blessing if they accept the gift of salvation:

> You are all sons of God through faith in Christ Jesus, for all of you who were baptized into Christ have clothed yourselves with Christ. There is neither Jew nor Greek, slave nor free, male nor female, for you are all one in Christ Jesus. If you belong to Christ, then you are Abraham's seed, and heirs according to the promise. (Gal. 3:26–29 NKJV)

Jesus validated the blessings of Father Abraham through His humanity and His divinity. If He did not have Mary's DNA, he could not bruise the head of the serpent; and if He did not have the Spirit of God, the Father, He could not defeat sin. More than a thousand years after the Fall, God acknowledged the faith of Abraham, counted it for righteousness, and declared the blessing of all nations through him. Does that mean humankind no longer had dominion over the earth after the Fall? The answer is no. It means that his dominion could be contested, and we already know by whom. God does nothing according to slackness so He called out Abraham from his people and established him as the head of a chosen nation, solidifying what He already declared in the beginning: that man would have dominion over the earth.

By choosing a man who stayed true to the commandment of God and establishing a "peculiar people," God paved the way for Jesus to "spirit-proof" humankind's dominion. Jesus is unquestionably the seed of Abraham and Adam, and "the begotten Son of God in whom God the Father is well pleased."

It is of interest to the believer to see that nowhere in scripture does Satan question the humanity of Christ, although he tried to cast doubt on His divinity during the time of Jesus's temptation in the wilderness when the devil challenged Him to prove that He was the Son of God (Matthew 4:1–11). The outcome of the challenge was victorious for Christ because He overcame the temptation of the devil by the word, and He did it while He was in human flesh

The lineage of Jesus is clearly passed down from Mary because she was His biological mother and Joseph was not his biological father. However, Joseph's position as his legal father was not nullified. Although Jesus boasts a royal heritage through Mary, who was a descendant of King David, Joseph gave him even greater credence in the earthly sense because he too was a descendant of King David. Establishing Christ's heritage through Joseph supports the cornerstone of Jewish culture since a child gained his identity, rights, and privileges from his patriarchal, not his matriarchal, lineage. Matthew traced the ancestry of Jesus from Abraham to Joseph to convince his Jewish readers that Jesus was the true Messiah and also to emphasize our Savior's right to be the redeemer of humanity (Matt. 1:1–17). On the other hand, Luke traced Jesus's genealogy in reverse order from Joseph to Adam to stress the fact that Christ was not only a descendant of the first human being but also the rightful heir of the Jewish patriarch, and that all the rights and privileges that God had promised Abraham culminated in Christ's coming to earth (Luke 3:23–38).

While Joseph cemented Christ's right to humanity, the Virgin Mary set Him apart from every man born from a woman. There is no human being, except Christ, who has not been engendered by the natural copulation between a man and woman or, in postmodern times, by artificial insemination of a female egg and a male sperm. Adam and Eve do not fit in either of those two categories since they were fashioned by the hand of God from the dust of the earth. Mary, who came from the priestly line of Aaron (we know that because she was the cousin of Elizabeth who we are told was a descendant of Aaron), had to be untouched by man if Jesus were to be sinless. Had Joseph been the biological father of Jesus, sin would have entered into him because all humanity was prone to sin after Adam rebelled against God in the garden. Through the woman, Eve, Satan deceived humankind, but through the obedience and simple faith of a young virgin, God outwitted the devil.

However, this young virgin had not attained the position of being the most blessed among women by herself. She had ridden on the boldness and faith of great women before her time, such as Sarah, Rebekah, Tamar, Rahab, Ruth, and other women who dared to do acts that not only quietly changed the face of history but also had powerful spiritual implications. None of these women have been mentioned in history books as important figures, yet their actions have impacted historical and political events over many generations and on different continents.

Nobody mentions the name of Sarah when we hear about the longstanding animosity between the Jews and the Arabs, although this Jewish matriarch's skepticism and lack of trust in Yahweh caused her to encourage her husband to commit one of the greatest errors in biblical history, which has deep ramifications even today. Abraham, swayed by his wife's advice, slept with Sarai's maidservant, Hagar, who conceived and bore a son called Ishmael. Sarai had not foreseen the tangled web she had woven until she noticed that after being impregnated by Abraham, her servant girl no longer had a demure demeanor in her presence but looked at her with scorn. Hagar's behavior was only a harbinger of what would develop into the most complicated feud of all times, and its effects transcend the borders of Asia, Europe, and North America.

Moreover, three dominant monotheistic religions have spread to nearly all corners of the earth: Judaism, Christianity, and Islam. In Ur of the Chaldeans, where polytheism was practiced, Abram and Sarai would have worshipped various gods, especially the moon god Nanna, who was also the patron saint of that city. None of the gods that Abram worshipped had spoken to him and affected his thinking like Jehovah. This God was so formidable that Abram had to forsake all other gods and commit to the will of this one God; hence the beginning of Judaism, which would culminate with the arrival of Moses who would receive God's commandments, which laid the foundation for Jewish religious, legal, political, and social infrastructures. This religion was created mainly for the Jews and not for other nations, so God had to fulfill his plan by ushering a religion that complemented the existing one if all nations were going to be blessed through Abram and humankind would be redeemed from sin. God therefore sent Christ to earth so the Jews could be released from the "harness" of the law of Judaism, and through them all other nations would receive salvation through faith. The story is that the Jews rejected salvation through faith and clave to the law of Judaism.

Today, although Judaism is the bedrock of Christianity, adherents of the two religions, though not enemies, contend over the deity of Christ, His death, and His resurrection. Islam, on the other hand, was birthed in dissent. Ishmael, the son of Hagar and Abram, was cast out of his father's home at the request of Sarah. Consequently, the bitterness that developed between the legal heir of Abram and his "illegitimate" son has continued throughout the centuries and has strongly impacted the Islamic religion and culture. The word *illegitimate* is used loosely here since the child born of a surrogate mother was legally considered the child of the wife of the master of a household and due certain rights under the law. Since the mother was the property of her master, she also had a legal right to share in familial benefits. Generally, the status of the concubine and her child was inferior to the privileges of the wife and her offspring. Sarah's act of expelling her servant and her child appear to be a heinous decision; however, Roland Kenneth Harrison in his *Introduction to the Old Testament* (1969) mentions that Sarah's action may not have been entirely unconscionable:

> [her] action could be defended according to the ancient Sumerian code of Lipit-Ishtar (ca. 1850 BC), one of the sources underlying the legislation of Hammurabi which stated that the

freedom received by the dispossessed slave was to be considered adequate compensation for the act of expulsion. (109)

Apparently, Sarah may have been aware of this loophole in the law and used it to her own advantage. She truly had the fury of a woman scorned, though not by her husband, as well as the heightened instincts of a mother who is aware that her offspring is in danger. Knowing that she had the power and justification to remove the object of her fury and protect the security of her only son, she exercised that power swiftly without any remorse. Although she had initiated the action that caused the birth of Ishmael, perhaps she also realized that if God's word was to be fulfilled, Hagar and her son had to be physically separated from Sarah's son, Isaac.

As awful as Sarah's action may seem in the exile of Ishmael and Hagar, God sanctioned it, though not for the same reasons that influenced her behavior. God had already told Abraham that his descendants would originate from his natural heir and that God's word was and is immutable, so He permitted Sarah's directive to be realized. However, He also blessed Ishmael because he was Abraham's seed. Although God upheld his promises to Abraham regarding Isaac, He did not stop the bitterness between Ishmael and Isaac and their seed, which resulted as an inevitable consequence of Abraham's preemptive act of begetting another son outside of God's covenant with him. Despite the fact that by her selfish action, Sarah unwittingly sowed the seeds of discord between two nations that would spring from Abraham, through grace she superseded her own faith and gave birth to the son of promise in her old age. As a result of this grace, she is counted in the annals of faith in Hebrews 11 as "a champion of faith." That woman is Sarah, matriarch of the Jewish nation.

CHAPTER 3

Sarai/Sarah

When Yahweh called out Abram to leave his kindred and go to a strange place, he had already chosen a wife. Her name was Sarai. In fact, she was his half-sister and extremely beautiful. Abram must have been the envy of many men because he was the husband of such a beautiful woman. Abram, in fact, conspired with Sarai on several occasions, saying that she was his sister and not his wife because he feared that he could be killed by other men who desired her because of her almost unsurpassed beauty. In Genesis 12:10–15, Abram allowed his fear to overcome him during his sojourn in the land of Egypt, and he encouraged Sarai to deceive Pharaoh. She lied to the latter and caused him to take her to his palace, but God in his mercy prevented him from sleeping with her.

> And there was a famine in the land: and Abram went down into Egypt to sojourn there; for the famine was grievous in the land. And it came to pass, when he was come near to enter into Egypt, that he said unto Sarai his wife, Behold now, I know that thou art a fair woman to look upon: Therefore it shall come to pass, when the Egyptians shall see thee, that they shall say, This is his wife: and they will kill me, but they will save thee alive. Say, I pray thee, thou art my sister: that it may be well with me for thy sake; and my soul shall live because of thee. And it came to pass, that, when Abram was come into Egypt, the Egyptians beheld the woman that she was very fair. The

princes also of Pharaoh saw her, and commended her before Pharaoh: and the woman was taken into Pharaoh's house. (Gen. 12:10–15 NKJV)·

Later in Adam's journey, he repeated the lie that he had told Pharaoh to King Abimelech. He told the king that she was his sister, and the king sent for her to be brought to his home. God intervened again and prevented the king from touching Sarai. Though Sarai may have been the envy of many women for her undeniable pulchritude, she bore the mark of sterility. Sarai was unable to provide an heir for her beloved husband. Abram had accumulated considerable wealth and prestige and wanted a natural son to inherit his possessions. He could not ignore the fact that he was aging. When he left Haran, he was already seventy-five years old, and by the time of the birth of Ishmael, Abram was eighty-six years old. God had told him more than once during that period that he would have a natural heir who would come from his wife, Sarai, but with the passing of each year, such declaration seemed more and more impossible.

Abram believed that God would provide an heir and God took note of his faith, according to Genesis 15:6 (KJV): "And he believed in the Lord; and he counted it to him for righteousness." However, like many of us today, his faith wavered because the promise was not manifested in the time that he had hoped. He struggled with doubts because reality belied the message of God's promise. One can imagine that when he sat with his wife in his tent, she had asked him about God's promise and why he continued to believe something that was humanly impossible. Most likely, he had to reassure her over and over again that he believed the words of this God because He was different from the gods of his fathers.

There were no records or precedent that he could cite to prove to his wife that her aging body could still produce a child. Perhaps he understood the shame that she bore knowing she was barren. In the ancient culture of Abram, it was almost like a curse for a woman to be sterile, especially one who was the wife of an influential man. Abram loved his wife very much and yearned to satisfy her desire to have a child. Perhaps his longing to give her the desires of her heart outweighed his own yearning for an heir. Obviously Abram struggled with the desire to please God and to please his wife. No wonder God, knowing that he was "only dust," visited him more than once to remind him of his promise and to strengthen his faith.

God already knew the heart of Sarai and that it would be easier for Abram to believe His word than for his wife to do the same. It was to Abram that God had appeared and told to leave his country, his friends, and relatives without knowing where he was going. It was also to Abram that He had given his promises; Sarai received the words of God through the reported speech of her husband. Even in a postmodern society with access to cell phones and the Internet in nearly every place on our planet, it would be emotionally disturbing for any wife to leave the comfort of friends and family and go to a remote place. The Ur of the Chaldeans, where they had lived before coming to Haran, was a well-known city of political and commercial importance, and Haran, although not as famous as the former city, was also well known.

Who knows the thoughts that were going through Sarai's mind as her otherwise level-headed husband tried to explain that they were going to leave Haran because an "unknown" God told him to do so but had not told him exactly where he was going. Not only would this unknown God reveal their destination after their departure but He also promised Abram that he would be the father of a great nation and through him all nations of the earth would be blessed. How could this be when Sarai had not borne any children yet? Although she was not very old, she was past the traditional age when most women in her culture would have had their first child. She would have been sixty-five years old then because Abram was seventy-five years old when he left his home country.

Regardless of her incredulity about Adam's encounter with the unknown God, Sarai had known her husband long enough to know that in order for him to make such a serious decision, he had to be convinced that this God was credible. Both she and Abram knew how dangerous their journey could be; yet she submitted fully to his authority:

> It was thus that Sarah obeyed Abraham [following his guidance and acknowledging his headship over her by] calling him lord (master, leader, authority). (1 Peter 3:6 AMP).

How brave she was! She left the comfort of her familiar surroundings and her parents, relatives, and friends to go to an unknown destination with an apparently crazy husband. Other than her husband, the only kin she had to talk to was the wife of Lot, Abram's sole relative, who had left Haran with them. However, Lot decided to part company and settle in a pleasant region because the existing land could not contain all the animals and other possessions he and Abraham had acquired. Therefore, the only other females with whom Sarai could communicate were her maidservants, and it would be unlikely that she would discuss her personal concerns or fears with her subordinates. Apparently, servants were the property of their masters and had no rights. Sarai encouraged her husband to sexually exploit her servant Hagar to become the surrogate mother of the heir that she was unable to produce. Then Sarai mistreated her when she noticed that Hagar's attitude toward her had changed from humility to scorn. Although impregnation of a servant by her master may seem barbaric to our twenty-first century sensibility, note that Abram was not obligated to solicit Hagar's consent in order to have sexual intercourse with her. Although morally wrong, ancient Assyrian writings on marriage law show that a master could sleep with his female slave if his wife was unable to bear children. The child of that union would be the son or daughter of the master and his wife and would have all the rights and privileges of the natural heir. Obviously, if a son were born to the wife, then the rights and privileges of the servant's son would be subordinate to that of the legal heir. Since Hagar was considered property, Abram had the authority to use her for sexual services. However, Abram did not have divine right to sleep with Hagar; and although God blessed him, there were negative consequences for his actions.

Like Adam, Abram did not question the wisdom of his wife's request; he made his decision without consulting God. This action on the part of Abram and his wife tells us that although Abram had had encounters with Jehovah, there were remnants of his pagan religion and culture that he would have to shed as he learned the ways of his new God. He had to surrender resorting to deception, which he had used on several occasions, if he were to convince his wife that his relationship with this God was completely different from their experience with former gods. To help her grow in faith and reach the place where she would trust his God to fulfill His word in making her the mother of a great nation, he had to submit his will to him.

There are obvious parallels between Sarah and Eve: The two women encouraged their husbands to commit an act that was outside of God's will, both developed enmity between themselves and the one with whom they had sinned, and both caused a form of separation to take place that had far-reaching effects on people outside of their local sphere. Both of their actions triggered a domino effect that set off reverberations in the physical and spiritual realms that still affect humankind today.

Like Eve before her, Sarai allowed Satan to use her selfish desires, though unwittingly, to thwart God's plan for humanity. Eve lusted after the forbidden fruit in the garden, and Satan appealed to her lust of the eye to cause her to rebel against God. Satan more implicitly used Sarai's yearning for a son to entrap her in exploiting her maidservant to become a surrogate mother. However, her ostensibly harmless plan backfired because as soon as Hagar became pregnant with Abram's son, she despised her mistress.

> Now Sarai Abram's wife bare him no children: and she had an handmaid, an Egyptian, whose name was Hagar. And Sarai said unto Abram, Behold now, the Lord hath restrained me from bearing: I pray thee, go in unto my maid; it may be that I may obtain children by her. And Abram hearkened to the voice of Sarai. (Gen. 16:1–2 KJV)

Sarah suggested giving her servant to lie with Abram, but the scriptures do not record that he offered any objections. It was not unusual, however, in Abraham's culture for wives to turn over their servants to their husbands as concubines if they were unable to conceive. Harrison points to the custom that had its basis in Nuzu law and was practiced by the inhabitants of northern Mesopotamia from where Abraham originated:

> The normal marriage contract often made provision for such contingency [childlessness] by requiring a childless wife to supply her husband with a concubine by whom he could obtain an heir. (1969, 107–108)

Even slaves were adopted into families as sons and given the family name. No wonder Abram had considered adopting his loyal servant Eliezer as his son. He abandoned the idea after God told him that his heir would be his biological child, even before his wife had approached him with the idea of sleeping with Hagar. Why shouldn't he help God to speed up the fulfillment of his promise? After all, God said the child would come from his own loins, but He did not say he would come from Sarai. He did not realize then that God's ways are higher than our ways. Had he prayed about Sarai's request, he would have seen that her desire was motivated by the pride of life. Paul described the conception and birth of Ishmael as an act "after the flesh" in contrast to the birth of Isaac, which he noted was by promise:

> For it is written, that Abraham had two sons, the one by a bondmaid, the other by a freewoman. But he who was of the

bondwoman was born after the flesh; but he of the freewoman was by promise. (Gal. 4:22–23 KJV)

It took the evolving faith of Sarai to submit her aging body to be impregnated by Abraham because she was beyond the age of childbearing. God had the power to open her womb, but He waited until the appointed time when He knew that she and Abram were spiritually ready. Abram and Sarai had to learn the ways of God and learn to trust Him before God would provide a legitimate heir for them. He marked the time of fulfillment of His promise by changing Sarai's name to Sarah and Abram's name to Abraham.

Sarah had already shown by her preemptive act of encouraging her husband to lie with her maidservant that she was not ready for God's great purpose. Because she lacked the faith to wait for God's promise, she succumbed to her own natural desire to satisfy her husband's need for an heir. An heir, even if he was borne by her servant, would help her save face. That she would be scorned by her own maidservant was the farthest thing from her mind.

Had she considered the potential rivalry that would exist between Hagar and her, the enmity between Ishmael and Isaac, and the perpetual strife that eludes amicable relations between the Arabs and the Jews; perhaps Sarah would not have sent her husband into the arms of another woman. God predicted the root of aggression in Ishmael that would ignite the flames of dissension between his seed and Isaac's seed, just as he had told the serpent about the enhanced conflict between his seed and the woman's seed that would culminate in Christ's triumph over Satan after he died and rose again.

So the Lord God said to the serpent: "Because you have done this, You are cursed more than all cattle, And more than every beast of the field; On your belly you shall go, And you shall eat dust All the days of your life. And I will put enmity Between you and the woman, And between your seed and her Seed; He shall bruise your head, And you shall bruise His heel." *(*Gen. 3:14–15 KJV)

Likewise, God forewarned Hagar about the violence that her son would perpetrate against others and also the violence that would be perpetuated against him:

> And the angel of the Lord said unto her, Behold, thou art with child and shalt bear a son, and shalt call his name Ishmael; because the LORD hath heard thy affliction. And he will be a wild man; his hand will be against every man, and every man's hand against him; and he shall dwell in the presence of all his brethren. And she called the name of the Lord that spake unto her, Thou God seest me: for she said, Have I also here looked after him that seeth me? (Gen.16:11–13 KJV)

Like Sarah, if Abraham had foreseen the magnitude of his and Sarah's actions today, he would have opposed his wife's request to sleep with Hagar. He would not have had to make a distinction between two sons that came from his loins. Although Isaac was his legal heir, Ishmael was his firstborn. The latter was born at a time when Abraham needed to be reminded of his virility and he had the unconditional love of a father for his child. At the request of his wife, Abraham was forced to send Ishmael away after Isaac was born, but his love for his firstborn never diminished. One can only imagine the emotional turmoil that he experienced when he had to send Ishmael away.

> And Sarah saw the son of Hagar the Egyptian, which she had born unto Abraham, mocking. Wherefore she said unto Abraham, Cast out this bondwoman and her son: for the son of this bondwoman shall not be heir with my son, even with Isaac. And the thing was very grievous in Abraham's sight because of his son. And God said unto Abraham, Let it not be grievous in

thy sight because of the lad, and because of thy bondwoman; in all that Sarah hath said unto thee, hearken unto her voice; for in Isaac shall thy seed be called. And also of the son of the bondwoman will I make a nation, because he is thy seed. And Abraham rose up early in the morning, and took bread, and a bottle of water, and gave it unto Hagar, putting it on her shoulder, and the child, and sent her away: and she departed, and wandered in the wilderness of Beersheba. (Gen. 21:9–14 KJV)

However, he obeyed God and expelled Hagar and his Ishmael. This act of obedience was the harbinger of the ultimate test that God would require of Abraham: sacrificing Isaac.

By faith Abraham, when he was tried, offered up Isaac: and he that had received the promises offered up his only begotten son, Of whom it was said, That in Isaac shall thy seed be called: Accounting that God was able to raise him up, even from the dead; from whence also he received him in a figure. (Heb. 11:17–19 KJV)

The depth of his love for Ishmael was revealed after God reiterated His promise to give him a son from his wife, Sarah, and he pleaded with God in Genesis 17:18 (KJV), "O that Ishmael might live before thee!" Although he had the desire to adopt Ishmael as his heir, God had made it clear to him that his heir would come from his wife, Sarah, and not from another woman.

And God said, Sarah thy wife shall bear thee a son indeed; and thou shalt call his name Isaac: and I will establish my covenant with him for an everlasting covenant, and with his seed after him. (Gen.17:19 KJV)

Abraham must have had mixed feelings after hearing God's word. He may have felt elated to know that God would give him an heir from his beloved Sarah, but the sheer impossibility of her becoming impregnated and giving birth at her age made him fearful. It was not an easy decision for Abraham to expel Hagar and Ishmael from his home for reasons other than his love for his first son.

Harrison, in his *Introduction to the Old Testament,* presents two valid ones:

> The apprehension that Abraham felt when Sarah expressed her determination to expel Hagar and Ishmael (Gen. 21:11) was prompted as much by the knowledge that such action was in direct contravention of Nuzu law and social custom as by purely humanitarian considerations. (1969, 109)

Regardless of the mental turmoil Abraham experienced, God made it clear to him that the child of the flesh and the child of promise could not coexist (Gen. 21:12). As we already read in Galatians chapter 4, we know that Hagar represents the old covenant of the Mosaic law and Sarah represents the new covenant of grace that Christ brought. The two covenants are inherently contrary to each other; thus, there is a war between them. Jesus talked about the problem of trying to combine old legalism and new grace:

> Then He spoke a parable to them: "No one puts a piece from a new garment on an old one; otherwise the new makes a tear, and also the piece that was take out of the new does not match the old. And no one puts new wine into old wineskins; or else the new wine will burst the wineskins and be spilled, and the wineskins will be ruined. But new wine must be put into new wineskins, and both are preserved. (Luke 5:36–37 NKJV)

The physical act of the veil of the temple being ripped in twain during Christ's crucifixion was also a symbolic separation of the old and new. No more did man have to go to a high priest to intercede for him, but through faith he could go directly to God. Christ's blood made it possible for humanity to be forgiven.

We learn some basic things from the story of Abraham and Sarah: that sin brings separation, God's promises are immutable, God is merciful, and our actions have physical and spiritual implications. How often we underestimate God's emphasis on the fidelity of covenant! Abraham made a big error when he failed to believe that God would give him an heir outside of the covenant relationship of marriage. God instituted marriage in the garden of Eden between Adam and Eve for procreation and perpetuation of the human race, and God never breaks His own law.

God blessed Hagar and Ishmael because He had told Abraham that his seed would be numberless and all nations of the earth would be blessed through him. God did not condone the action of Adam and his wife, but He knew that Abraham had a heart to serve Him because he believed the initial promise of God and acted on it. Abraham manifested such extraordinary faith when he took the word of an unknown God and left his homeland without knowing his destination, even if he did not display that same faith when he took matters into his own hands and impregnated Hagar. How could it be that one of such great faith could engage in such folly? The answer lies in what Paul wrote centuries after the death of the patriarch:

> For I know that in me (that is, in my flesh) dwelleth no good thing: for to will is present with me; but how to perform that which is good I find not. For the good that I would I do not: but the evil which I would not, that I do. Now if I do that I would not, it is no more I that do it, but sin that dwelleth in me. I find then a law, that, when I would do good, evil is present with me. For I delight in the law of God after the inward man: But I see another law in my members, warring against the law of my mind, and bringing me into captivity to the law of sin which is

in my members. O wretched man that I am! who shall deliver me from the body of this death? (Rom, 7:18–24 NKJV)

Abraham and Sarah did not have the guidance of the Mosaic law or the illumination of the Word through Jesus Christ. They gained knowledge as God revealed it to them and as they grew in faith over the course of time. The faith of Adam provided the one who would deliver wretched humankind from "the body of this death" that Paul describes. Humankind died a spiritual death after Adam and Eve sinned. God had made them a little lower than the angels and crowned them with glory and honor (Heb. 2:7). They would be totally dependent on their Maker and would enjoy all the blessings that God prepared for them before the world began. Disobedience changed the course of God's plan, but divine omniscience provided a way of escape for us through the obedience of Abraham and Sarah.

Often we hear about the faith of Abraham, but we know that behind every successful man is a good woman. Sarah, with all her flaws, served her husband well. She had left her home with him on what some would describe as a wild-goose chase, based solely on what he claimed was the word of a strange god. She had placed herself in danger on several occasions in order to protect Abraham and ultimately produced the son he had yearned for in her old age. Of all three women with whom Abraham was associated, including Hagar and Keturah,[1] Sarah had pride of place. She was the one chosen to be the mother of all nations and is hailed in the Christian "Hall of Faith" as a beacon of faith.

> Through faith also Sarah herself received strength to conceive seed, and was delivered of a child when she was past age, because she judged him faithful who had promised. Therefore sprang there even of one, and him as good as dead, so many as the stars

---

[1.] Keturah was Abraham's concubine whom he took as his wife after the death of Sarah. See Genesis 25:1–6 and 1 Chronicles 1:32.

of the sky in multitude, and as the sand which is by the sea shore innumerable. (Heb.1:11–12 NKJV)

We can therefore say that Abraham's biography would have been completely different had there not been a Sarah. Her beauty, fearlessness, trust, faith, love, fallibility, and even her infertility worked together for good in shaping the life of a man whom God called his friend:

But thou, Israel, art my servant, Jacob whom I have chosen, the seed of Abraham my friend. (Isa.41:8 NKJV)

CHAPTER 4

Rebekah

Sarah was one hundred and twenty-seven years old when she died and did not live to see the wife of her son Isaac. However, she had lived long enough to see him reach adulthood and must have been aware that he would need a wife in order to continue the Abrahamic line and honor the covenant relationship that God had established with his father. He was the child that lifted her shame of barrenness, and besides, he was the only son, so naturally she doted on him. Therefore, she would be meticulous about choosing a wife for him. She must have talked to him about the covenant that God had made with his father, Abraham, and the importance of not becoming involved with the Canaanite women who were living among them.

How great her joy would be to see the girl who became her son's wife! She had laughed with happiness at Isaac's birth, an infectious laugh that she hoped would motivate others who heard her to laugh with her (Gen. 21:6). She would have been pleased that God had granted Isaac a wife who met all the requirements that Abraham had desired in the woman that would be the mother of his legal heir. We glean from Genesis 24:67 that Isaac shared a very close relationship with his mother and had experienced deep grief after her death and needed a diversion to help him cope with his loss.

> And Isaac brought her into his mother Sarah's tent, and took
> Rebekah, and she became his wife; and he loved her: and Isaac
> was comforted after his mother's death. (Gen. 24:67 KJV)

The chemistry between Rebekah and Isaac was spontaneous, and to say
that it was a relationship made in heaven is not an exaggeration. After
Sarah died, Abraham had the responsibility of finding the perfect wife
for Isaac, so he instructed his eldest and most trusted servant to return to
his homeland to his extended family to seek a woman among them. He
insisted that Isaac's wife must be taken from his own extended family
because he did not want his son to be corrupted by the pagan ways of
the women in Canaan. Abraham took the seriousness of the covenant
that God had made with him, and he promised that his seed would be
blessed and that through him all nations of the earth would be blessed.
Therefore, he would not take any risks in jeopardizing the execution of
the covenant relationship. At that stage in his life, he had learned from
the mistake he had made with Hagar. Abraham was so protective of
the covenant relationship he had with God that he told his servant if he
was not successful in finding a wife in Haran, he should not bring back
Isaac to Canaan. He made the decision knowing that perhaps he would
not see his son again before his death, but he was willing to surrender
his desires to remain faithful to the will of God.

However, his worst fears were not realized because God knew the
desires of His friend's heart and granted him his wish. God had already
declared in Genesis 18:19 that He knew Abraham would be faithful
to Him; therefore, God was gracious and revealed His plan to him to
destroy Sodom and Gomorrah in order to save Abraham's nephew, Lot,
and his family.

> For I know him, that he will command his children and his
> household after him, and they shall keep the way of the Lord,
> to do justice and judgment; that the Lord may bring upon
> Abraham that which he hath spoken of him. (Gen. 18:19 KJV)

After Abraham's trusted servant left on his journey to fulfill his master's plan, he called on the God of Abraham to help him with the great responsibility with which he had been entrusted. He had been with Abraham for most of his life, so he had seen how Yahweh had blessed his master. Here was a perfect opportunity to test this God himself. He prayed and asked the God of Abraham to grant him the wish of his master and to show him a sign so he would know his prayer had been answered. It did not take long for God to grant his request. The answer to that prayer was Rebekah. She was truly a part of Abraham's kindred, the grandniece of both Abraham and Sarah. She was the granddaughter of Nahor and Milcah, brother and niece of Abraham and Sarah.

Rebekah showed no hesitation when her relatives asked her if she would leave them and go to a strange country to become the wife of a man she had not met. When Sarah left Mesopotamia, she was already married to Abraham and could trust him to protect her even if she was not sure where he was going. Rebekah, on the other hand, was aware of her destination although she had never visited Canaan. However, she was putting her trust in the servant of the man she was going to marry whom she had never met. Although the Bible does not mention that Yahweh had spoken to Rebekah as He had done with Abraham, based on the events leading up to her meeting with Isaac, we can be certain that He had prepared her heart for her marriage to Isaac and separation from her loved ones. Rebekah's parents and brother gave their approval for her marriage, but they did not coerce her into accepting the offer. They surmised that it was executed by divine intervention and Rebekah would be compliant; therefore, they blessed her:

> And they said, We will call the damsel, and enquire at her mouth. And they called Rebekah, and said unto her, Wilt thou go with this man? And she said, I will go. And they sent away Rebekah their sister, and her nurse, and Abraham's servant, and his men. And they blessed Rebekah, and said unto her, Thou

art our sister, be thou the mother of thousands of millions, and let thy seed possess the gate of those which hate them. And Rebekah arose, and her damsels, and they rode upon the camels, and followed the man: and the servant took Rebekah, and went his way. (Gen 24:57–61 KJV)

Isaac was forty years old and at the height of his manhood when he married Rebekah. He yearned for love and female companionship, especially now that his mother was dead. He could not communicate as much as he desired with people of his own age because most of those living in his household were servants of his father and there were barriers to his relationship with them because of the difference in their social status. Although Abraham had fathered other children from his concubines, Isaac was his only heir; therefore, he did not share a natural kinship with his other "siblings." Moreover, his father was a foreigner in the place where they lived and he had little in common with the inhabitants. His father's loyalty to his God prevented him from assimilating into the culture of the region where he lived.

Isaac fell in love with Rebekah at first sight. She was as beautiful as his mother and appeared healthy enough to bear sons to preserve his father's bloodline. However, his and Abraham's dreams for sons and grandsons were to be deferred for a long time because Sarah would remain barren for many years.

In spite of his longing for children, Isaac did not repeat the error of his father in seeking an heir outside of his covenant relationship with Rebekah. Instead he inquired of the Lord and God opened her womb. Isaac had been old enough to know that Abraham had attempted to sacrifice him at the bidding of Yahweh, and just before his father was about to plunge the knife into his son's chest, God called out from heaven and restrained him. He had seen how God had miraculously provided a ram in his place and how his terror subsided as his father loosened him from the makeshift altar where he had placed him. He later learned after that God had commanded Abraham to sacrifice his only son to prove his allegiance to Him. Perhaps Isaac thought that the Lord was testing him as he had tested his father. His parents had always told him that God was mysterious in his ways and had reiterated many times the miracle of his own conception.

Not only did God allow Rebekah to be impregnated but he also blessed her with twins who struggled in her womb. The young mother was perplexed by the unusual convulsions inside her stomach, so she also inquired of the Lord about them. God informed her that the babes in her womb represented two different nations, and one group would be stronger than the other group. Moreover, the elder child would serve the younger. This revelation must have been startling to Rebekah and Isaac. They were elated to know that they would have children, but to realize that their children could eventually become enemies and that the older would serve the younger was overwhelming. According to the law of primogeniture, the firstborn child, usually a son, inherited most, if not all, of his parents' estate, assumed more responsibility, and received more honor than his younger siblings. Isaac and Rebekah had every intention of following the conventions of what their parents had taught them about raising children, so they were unsure how God's predictions would play out in the lives of their offspring.

It did not take long for God's word to start being fulfilled. Rebekah and Isaac would later realize that what had occurred in the womb was a foreshadowing of other experiences in the lives of their sons that had deep spiritual implications. During the time of Rebekah's delivery, as the first twin came through the birth canal, the other twin came out and clutched the heel of his brother with his hand. The name of the first twin was Esau, and the second was Jacob. Genesis 25:25 notes that Esau was red and hairy all over and that Jacob grabbed his brother's heel because mention of the physical and mental characteristics of the twins would later be significant factors in the loss of Esau's birthright to his younger brother, Jacob.

> And when her days to be delivered were fulfilled, behold, there
> were twins in her womb. And the first came out red, all over
> like an hairy garment; and they called his name Esau. And after
> that came his brother out, and his hand took hold on Esau's heel;
> and his name was called Jacob: and Isaac was threescore years
> old when she bare them. (Gen. 25:24–26 KJV)

Although Rebekah and Isaac loved their two sons, they committed a
grave error by showing acts of favoritism to each one. Isaac showed
more love toward Esau because the boy had an affinity for the outdoors
and was a skillful hunter who was able to provide venison for the family.
On the other hand, Jacob was more domesticated and received more
affection from his mother.

> And the boys grew: and Esau was a cunning hunter, a man of
> the field; and Jacob was a plain man, dwelling in tents. And
> Isaac loved Esau, because he did eat of his venison: but Rebekah
> loved Jacob. (Gen. 25:27–28 KJV)

Unfortunately, both parents did not just express random acts of affection
toward their sons but showed favoritism to their preferred child. Since
Jacob loved to "dwell in the tents," he spent a lot a time with his mother
and therefore developed a very close relationship with her. Esau, though
he spent many hours outdoors, had adequate time with his father to create
a bond with him. The sharp distinctions in personality between the two
brothers not only caused marked differences in their parents' treatment
toward them but also forged the extraordinary course of their lives.

Esau's free spirit blended well with the wild, untamed outdoors.
Apparently he had the uneasy strength of a crouched lion waiting for
its prey. He was able to perceive when an animal was in his range and
then pounce. He had patience, the kind of patience that was on edge,
unlike that of his brother whose patience was wholly cerebral, having
been cultivated in the cool of his mother's tent.

They both were cunning. Esau had gleaned his from his days learning the ways of animals and nature, while Jacob observed human behavior and gained invaluable information from his mother because he spent more time at or close to home. Jacob also tended the sheep—a vocation that would serve him well in the future. He understood well the foibles of human nature and showed a better grasp of legal and political matters than his impetuous older brother. He transformed what may have been an innocuous exchange between two brothers into a formal binding agreement by soliciting Esau's sworn declaration to uphold its terms and ultimately usurping his brother's position with the help of his mother. His grandfather, Abraham, had set a precedent for him when he made his servant Eliezer swear to him that he would not take a wife for Isaac from the "daughters of the Canaanites, but from Abraham's own kindred."

> And Abraham said unto his eldest servant of his house, that ruled over all that he had, Put, I pray thee, thy hand under my thigh: And I will make thee swear by the Lord, the God of heaven, and the God of the earth, that thou shalt not take a wife unto my son of the daughters of the Canaanites, among whom I dwell: But thou shalt go unto my country, and to my kindred, and take a wife unto my son Isaac. (Gen. 24:2–4 KJV)

Jacob was handy around the house, even showing some culinary ability. Thanks to his mother, he had learned to cook the kind of stew that would cause his famished brother's mouth to water. Esau had returned home from one of his frequent hunting trips, and he was as ravenous as the wolves he had encountered in the forest. He felt like he had no time to wait for the meat that he brought home to be dressed and cooked; therefore, he begged his younger brother to give him a bowl of his red pottage stew. His brother promised to give it to him in exchange for his birthright. How could anyone even ask to exchange something so priceless for something of little value? The answer is that Jacob coveted his brother's position, and Esau's hunger provided the perfect opportunity to take from him what he had wanted for a long time.

What he lacked in physical prowess was compensated for by his wits. He also had a profound understanding of primogeniture: the rights, privileges, and responsibilities of a firstborn son, and Esau did not.

There is truth in the belief that a man is at his wit's end when he is starving because Esau gave little thought to his brother's proposition and accepted his seemingly harmless request.

> And Jacob said, Sell me this day thy birthright. And Esau said, Behold, I am at the point to die: and what profit shall this birthright do to me? And Jacob said, Swear to me this day; and he sware unto him: and he sold his birthright unto Jacob. Then Jacob gave Esau bread and pottage of lentiles; and he did eat and drink, and rose up, and went his way: thus Esau despised his birthright. (Gen. 25:32–34 KJV)

Esau not only perfunctorily dismissed a custom that was steeped in honor, but he relinquished his birthright and all the rights, duties, and privileges pertaining to it. He did not consider that he had sealed his fate when he swore to Jacob. The practice of giving the eldest son a greater share of his parents' estate and privileges was not just to ensure that he had a good start after his parents' death but it also was a means of empowering a designee to be responsible for the preservation and well-being of the family. Therefore, the position was not to be taken lightly. However, Esau did not give it serious thought and hoped it would be forgotten as quickly as he ate the pottage. In Esau's family, his role would even be more significant than his peers because of the covenant that God had made with Abraham. His position therefore took on a priestly dimension as he was expected to carry out the directives of God and teach them to his household so God's purpose would be fulfilled on the earth.

Abraham had told his family about God's promises and had taught them to fear Him; therefore, Esau was not ignorant of his familial expectations. However, he showed contempt for what was sacred and concentrated on satisfying his carnal needs. His disregard for his birthright showed up even more after he married two Hittite women. His marriages were like a slap in the face to his parents, considering that his grandfather had gone to such extreme lengths to ensure that Isaac would marry a woman from his own people because he did not want his son to be influenced by the pagan practices of the people around him.

> And Esau was forty years old when he took to wife Judith the daughter of Beeri the Hittite, and Bashemath the daughter of Elon the Hittite: Which were a grief of mind unto Isaac and to Rebekah. (Gen. 26:34–35 KJV)

Other than Rebekah's obvious preference for Jacob, her disdain for Esau's wives may have motivated her to devise one of the greatest schemes in biblical history. God had already predicted that the older twin would serve his younger brother, but He had not told Rebekah how it would be done. Before the birth of her sons, it would not have crossed her mind that she would engineer the downfall of her own son, even if his loss of position seemed inevitable. After all, God had predicted that Jacob would be greater than his older brother, so she may have been wondering as they were growing up how this would happen. We will find out that the charming and demure girl whom we met in Genesis 24 would conspire with Jacob to bring this to pass. She could be a deceptive and ruthless woman, using Machiavellian tactics to get her desired end. She was determined that her favorite son would outrank his older brother and enjoy all the rights and privileges that should have been accorded to Esau because he was the firstborn son.

Her chance came when Isaac requested that Esau hunt for venison and prepare it for him so he could bless him before he died (Gen. 27, KJV). She overheard Isaac's words and intercepted his plan. She convinced Jacob to fetch two young goats from a nearby herd and prepare delicious meat for Isaac. She then covered the arms and neck of Jacob with the skins from the goats in order to make them feel like the hairy skin of Esau.

How ironic that Esau's body, which was "red, all over like an hairy garment" (Gen. 25:25 KJV) and acted as a buffer against the cold winds of the wild, would also make him a victim to the wiliness of his mother and brother!

Rebekah, knowing that Isaac was blind, resorted to using his sense of touch to identify his sons and deceived him. As she had anticipated, when Jacob brought the prepared meat to his father, Isaac smelled the goat's skin, touched his hairy hands, and was convinced that he was Esau. Consequently, he blessed Jacob with Esau's blessings. When Esau returned and brought the prepared venison, Isaac and Esau discovered that Jacob had stolen his brother's blessings. Esau realized he had dallied with his inheritance and lost everything.

Esau had been outwitted twice by Jacob: the first time he succumbed to his carnal desire for food, and the second time he was the victim of the schemes of his mother and brother. He was close to his father, but he loved his mother and could not have anticipated that she would plot to take away his inheritance. Rebekah had betrayed her husband's and son's trust although they were not aware of her duplicity. She initiated enmity between her two sons and therefore had to continue her web of deceit in order to protect Jacob from the wrath of Esau. Naturally, Esau became angry after he found out what Jacob had done to him, and he plotted to kill him.

Rebekah became aware of Esau's plan and planned to send Jacob to Laban, her brother, who lived in Paddan-Aram. She used her already known distaste for Hittite women as a red herring to disguise her true intention to send Jacob away. She appealed to her husband's fear by exaggerating the effect of the emotional turmoil she was experiencing living among Hittite women and how it could become a greater threat to her health if Jacob were to marry one of them. Esau had already married two of these women, and she knew Isaac was very displeased with his choice. As she anticipated, Isaac affirmed her decision, blessed Jacob, charged him not to marry the daughters of Canaan, and sent him to Mesopotamia.

The Bible did not reveal if Isaac found out that his wife instigated the "heist" for Esau's blessings, but what is revealed is that Rebekah was way ahead of her time. She was decisive and assertive—an apparent contrast to her husband, Isaac. Isaac is not considered weak, but there were instances in which he could have been assertive but refrained from taking action. For example, when Jacob disguised himself as Esau, Isaac noticed that although his skin was hairy like Esau's, his voice was not Esau's. However, he ignored the discrepancy between what he heard and what he felt, and went along with Jacob's hoax.

From what we know of Rebekah's personality, we can almost be sure that she would have probed deeper into the matter had she been the one in Isaac's shoes. Other than possessing great beauty, she was a woman who could think on her feet. It is noted in Genesis 26:6–11(KJV) that Isaac dwelled in the land of Gerar after the death of Abraham, and the men there lusted after Rebekah because she was "fair to look upon" (v. 7). When they inquired after her, Isaac lied that she was his sister because he was afraid they would kill him for her.

Rebekah, armed with beauty and skilled in the art of subterfuge and intrigue, could make any sophisticated twenty-first-century woman look like an ingenuous schoolgirl. However, she was not a villain. We catch glimpses of her kindness when she gave water not only to Abraham's servant but also to his camels and invited him to lodge at her home (Gen. 24:17–24). Her love for Esau may have been questionable, but she had affection for both sons. She expressed her fears about losing either of them after she found out that Esau was planning to kill Jacob.

And these words of Esau her elder son were told to Rebekah: and she sent and called Jacob her younger son, and said unto him, Behold, thy brother Esau, as touching thee, doth comfort himself, purposing to kill thee. Now therefore, my son, obey my voice; arise, flee thou to Laban my brother to Haran; And tarry with him a few days, until thy brother's fury turn away; Until thy brother's anger turn away from thee, and he forget that which thou hast done to him: then I will send, and fetch thee from thence: why should I be deprived also of you both in one day? (Gen. 27:42–45 KJV)

She had been divinely chosen and blessed by her family to become "the mother of thousands of millions" (Gen. 24:60). In spite of her human flaws, she believed in upholding the covenant that God had made with Abraham, and she was genuinely disappointed by Esau's marriage to Hittite women (Gen. 26:35).

Rebekah, like Sarah, intercepted the plan of God to satisfy her own will, which produced negative results. Her plot to steal Esau's blessing caused enmity between her two sons and started an ongoing conflict between the Israelites and the Edomites—just as Sarah's action to produce an heir without God's approval engendered animosity between Ishmael's descendants and the Jews. In 2 Samuel 8:14, it is recorded that the Edomites at one time served the Israelites when David extended his northern kingdom, fulfilling God's word that two kinds of people would come from Rebekah's womb and one group would be stronger than the other group (Gen. 25:23). The Edomites were descendants of Esau, and the Israelites were the descendants of Jacob. Genesis 25:30 indicates that Esau was called Edom after he ate the red pottage and sold his birthright to Jacob, hence the name "Edomites." God changed Jacob's name to Israel after He appeared to him at Bethel; therefore, his descendants were called Israelites (Gen. 35:10).

Although Esau had set in motion his own destiny by selling his birthright to Jacob and swearing to honor the terms of the oath, his act does not negate Rebekah's wrongdoing. However, his oath to his brother initiated a spiritual process that was manifested later. Hebrews 12:16–17 describes Esau as a "profane person" who gave up his birthright for "one morsel of meat" and afterward, when it was due for him to receive his blessing, was rejected because he had forfeited it at the time of surrendering his birthright. Therefore, when Isaac decided, at the end of his life, to bless his sons and unwittingly blessed Jacob with the blessings usually accorded to the firstborn son, he only performed in the natural realm what had already been sealed in the spiritual.

Esau was not the only one who would reap the effects of his and his mother's actions. Jacob too was to receive a mixed bag of blessings and curses throughout his life. He gained wealth and possessions, but he was tricked on several occasions and suffered extended emotional pain and hurt because he displayed the same favoritism in his own family that he had seen his parents show to him and his brother. Yet, despite Jacob's fallacies, God remembered his promise to Abraham and blessed him.

In the same way that God used Rebekah's son to carry out his purpose with all his imperfections, he had chosen her to be part of His covenant plan. It's easy to forget that she was blessed and favored by God because her life as a wife and mother reads as a saga of lies, deceit, and rivalry. It is also surprising that the death and burial of Rebekah's nurse Deborah was recorded in Genesis 35:8; yet nothing else was mentioned about Rebekah after she sent Jacob to Mesopotamia, except that she was buried with Isaac "in the cave that is in the field of Machpelah". Perhaps her final years were mostly spent in solitude and regret for some of the mistakes she had made, and also thanking God for giving her sons after years of infertility. One can only imagine the guilt that she felt for having deceived the man she loved and, perhaps, some remorse for the bitterness of Esau. She must have heard Esau's heart-wrenching screams after he realized that his blessings had been stolen.

And when Esau heard the words of his father, he cried with a great and exceeding bitter cry, and said unto his father, Bless me, even me also, O my father. (Gen. 27:34 KJV)

Although she did not suffer the physical loss of her children as she had feared, she must have suffered emotional loss. Her relationship with Esau was already strained because of his marriage to the daughters of Heth, and the ongoing favoritism she showed Jacob would have stirred up resentment even before he stole Esau's blessings. If there was any affection between Rebekah and Esau before Jacob stole his blessings, that tie was cut by Esau's obsession with avenging his brother. She also must have yearned for the presence of Jacob, whom she was forced to send away as a result of her own actions, and sometimes felt gratitude that God had spared the lives of her two sons.

Rebekah was not oblivious of Abraham's God because she consulted him when she experienced the unusual jostling of the twins in her womb and maybe for other reasons. Moreover, she knew how God had blessed her father-in-law as well as the divine intervention in her own marriage with Isaac and her miraculous conception with twins after an extended period of barrenness. Her story is the story of Sarah, Rachel, and other women who would play important roles in the birth and perpetuation of the Jewish nation. They are women joined and marred by the bloodline thread of their Adamic nature, but they were allowed to overcome their imperfections because the God who blew His breath into them remained connected to them and others who would come after them for the execution of His greater purpose.

CHAPTER 5

Rachel and Leah

Two for One

Jacob was on his way to his uncle's house when he met Rachel. He had stopped by a well that drew his attention because shepherds were gathered there with their flocks, but the mouth of the well was covered by a stone. He drew near and inquired from where they had come, and they told him they had come from Haran. Jacob was overjoyed because that was his destination, where his mother had sent him to stay with her brother, Laban. He found out from the men that his uncle was well and had a daughter who would soon arrive to water her father's flock. She arrived momentarily and Jacob wasted no time in gingerly rolling away the stone from the well's mouth and watering the maiden's flock. Jacob did not know whether he was overcome with joy at seeing one of his mother's relatives or by Rachel's stunning beauty because he was crying and kissing her fervently at the same time. In between gasps of delight and tears, Jacob told Rachel that he was the son of Rebekah, her father's sister, and the damsel ran home to tell her father the good news. After hearing the news, Laban ran to meet the son of his beloved Rebekah and welcomed him with open arms.

Jacob stayed with his uncle for about a month, and not to wear out his welcome, he helped his uncle with the daily tasks that were done by him and the men of his household. Jacob had been in a hurry when he left

Canaan, so he had no time to bring worldly possessions with him. Laban took notice, and not only offered to pay him for his work but also gave Jacob the chance to choose what he wanted for his wages. Jacob seized the opportunity to tell his uncle that he would serve him for seven years if he would permit him to marry Rachel. Jacob had fallen madly in love with her at first sight at the well. Rachel was the younger of his uncle's two daughters; she had such irresistible good looks that perhaps she enjoyed more attention than her seemingly less attractive older sister, Leah.

> And Laban had two daughters: the name of the elder was Leah, and the name of the younger was Rachel. Leah was tender eyed; but Rachel was beautiful and well favoured. And Jacob loved Rachel; and said, I will serve thee seven years for Rachel thy younger daughter. (Gen. 29:16–18 KJV)

Jacob loved her so much that seven years seemed like a short time to work for his bride. He looked forward to the day when she would be his and they could start a family and continue to the Abrahamic line. However, his dream would not be realized with Rachel because the woman he woke up with the morning after his wedding night was Leah, not his betrothed. His sins had caught up with him. The deceiver was outsmarted by his uncle, a man who was more experienced in the ways of the world than Jacob.

Jacob was crafty, but he had not been exposed to many things and had been disarmed by his uncle's apparent charm. How could he have underestimated the cunning of Laban when Laban's sister, his mother, was skillful in duplicity? As a matter of fact, it was because of Jacob's duplicity and that of Rebekah that he was in his uncle's home. Deception seemed to be a family trait that Jacob had to be rid of before he could enjoy the blessings of the Abrahamic covenant. By an ironic twist of fate, he saw again how one parent's trickery could reverse the order of familial entitlement and cause rivalry among siblings. Laban was a reminder of Jacob's past: he supplanted Leah for Rachel just as Jacob had supplanted Esau. Moreover, he told Jacob that the younger daughter was never allowed to marry before her older sister. How much truth there was in Laban's statement is uncertain, but it may have created a tinge of guilt in Jacob's mind to stop his protest. He should not have been surprised by his uncle's trickery—he was truly his mother's brother. Now that Jacob was not the creator of duplicity, but the victim, he emphatically expressed his dissatisfaction.

> And Laban gave his maid Zilpah to his daughter Leah as a maid. So it came to pass in the morning, that behold, it was Leah. And he said to Laban, "What is this you have done to me? Was it not for Rachel that I served you? Why then have you deceived me?" And Laban said, "It must not be done so in our country, to give the younger before the firstborn. Fulfill her week, and we will give you this one also for the service which you will serve with me still another seven years." (Gen. 29:24–27 KJV)

If Jacob felt guilty after Laban's trickery, his subsequent reaction did not support this emotion. He had no choice but to honor his marriage to Leah, but he was still determined to have Rachel as his wife too. He offered to work seven more years for Rachel and married her after fulfilling his week of marital obligation with Leah. God had appeared to Jacob in Bethel on his way to Paddan-Aram and reminded him of the promise he had made to Abraham and Isaac, yet he did not consult God before taking a second wife. He allowed the lust of the flesh and the eye to guide him to marry Rachel. Since he loved her more than Leah, he showed favoritism toward her and despised Leah. However, Genesis 29:31 tells us that God saw Leah's plight and made her fruitful, but He shut up Rachel's womb. While the two sisters were growing up in their father's house in Paddan-Aram, Leah was overlooked while Rachel was showered with attention.

Apparently, Rachel was blessed with a strong, beautiful body for childbearing, and Leah had the weak eye (perhaps not a good sign for producing sons). It also did not help Leah's self-esteem knowing that Jacob hated her. The names of some of her children tell the depth of her pain and triumph: Reuben, her firstborn, "The Lord hath taken away my sorrow"; Simeon, "The Lord has heard that my husband doesn't love me"; Levi, "Now my husband will hold me close"; and Judah, "I'll praise the Lord!" Leah ignited the jealousy and rage of her sister after giving birth to four sons. It must have been extremely hard for Rachel to swallow the fact that her sister Leah was taking attention from her because she was able to produce sons for Jacob. It didn't make sense that she was still her husband's favorite wife and she had not borne him any children. What shame she felt! His affection for her was not going to last, she must have thought, if her less attractive sister continued to be fruitful while she remained infertile.

In her frustration, Rachel turned her anger on her husband and incurred his wrath:

> And when Rachel saw that she bare Jacob no children, Rachel envied her sister; and said unto Jacob, Give me children, or else I die. And Jacob's anger was kindled against Rachel: and he said, Am I in God's stead, who hath withheld from thee the fruit of the womb? (Gen. 30:1–2, KJV)

Although angry with his wife, somewhere deep inside Jacob knew that God had closed the womb of his beloved Rachel; he was not oblivious to the stories of his grandmother and mother. His own mother, Rebekah, had suffered barrenness, as well as his grandmother Sarah. On both occasions God intervened and opened their wombs. Would God do that for Rachel although Jacob showed favoritism toward her? By a similar twist of fate, Rachel, like Sarah who was barren, intercepted God's plan and encouraged her husband to sleep with Bilhah, her servant. How history repeats itself! Jacob did not learn from his grandfather's error that he committed by impregnating Hagar, but he repeated what Abraham had done. Not only had he slept with each maidservant at the bidding of both Rachel and Leah but he also repeated the action. From these sexual encounters he begat four sons: Dan and Naphtali from Rachel's servant, Bilhah, and Gad and Asher from Leah's servant, Zilpah.

In contrast to Hagar's son, the children of Leah's and Rachel's servants remained part of Jacob's household and formed part of the twelve tribes of Israel. Despite the schemes, deception, rivalry, and hatred in Jacob's household, God still had compassion for them. He reopened the womb of Leah and gave her two more sons and a daughter after her servant had produced two sons, and He had mercy on Rachel and blessed her with a male child they named Joseph. Joseph later would play an integral role in the survival of his father and the preservation of the children of Israel. Again God blessed Rachel, and she gave birth to Benjamin. However, it was a mixed blessing because she died during labor.

Before their older cousin arrived in their city and received shelter in their home, Leah and Rachel seemed to be the only children of Laban. No doubt, as his sister's son and a strong male, Jacob was a welcome addition to his family. We only hear about Laban's sons after Jacob had been living with him for a number of years. Laban was a shepherd of considerable means because he owned land and servants. He gave both Leah and Rachel servant girls as wedding gifts when they married Jacob. The two servant girls became surrogate mothers for four of the children born to Jacob. Both sisters seemed to be industrious: Rachel, being younger and more energetic, tended the sheep while Leah remained at home, perhaps doing house chores because she was older and less vivacious than her beautiful sister.

Nothing tells us how often Leah had been overlooked by possible suitors because she did not have the striking good looks of her sister, but one thing was certain: her father was going to make sure that she would marry whether by fair means or foul. Laban was protective toward Leah because he did not want her to endure the ignominy and perhaps the agony of being a spinster. He believed that Rachel would not have problems finding a husband, and moreover, Jacob was so infatuated with her that perhaps he would work seven more years for her.

Rachel the Chosen

Rachel had no doubt that she was the apple of Jacob's eye. She had captured his heart, and he was going to have her by any means necessary. Before he completed his bridal week with Leah, he was already negotiating with Laban how he could acquire his beloved Rachel. The week could not be finished early enough before he was driven to her arms, and he frequented there while visiting Leah out of necessity. He was undaunted by the fact that he had to work seven more years for her in fulfillment of his promise to her father. In all, he worked fourteen years for her because he had not anticipated that his father-in-law would trick him after working the first seven years for her.

To have one's husband's full attention is the dream of every wife. Rachel was in an enviable position because Jacob's desire was toward her and not her sister. Why was she so jealous? Because in her society, according to Harrison, procreation was more valued than companionship in a marriage and "a married woman who proved to be unable to bear children for one reason or another was in an extremely invidious position" (1969, 107).

Children were a blessing and those who bore them were also considered blessed. Although Jacob had shown no less attention to Rachel than before, she was aware that he would not ignore the woman who bore him several sons. It seemed almost comical that her feebler sister would be her envy. She should have been happy for Leah, but in light of their circumstances, it was difficult. She was not willing to share Jacob with her sister, even if she was the "other wife." Jacob had chosen her and not Leah!

Mandrakes for hire

In the game of rivalry, reason takes a backseat and the winner takes all. After Leah's body took a hiatus from reproducing, she decided to give Mother Nature a helping hand. She gladly accepted mandrakes that her son Reuben had brought her from the field. Little did this young boy know that his innocent find would be bartered for sex. Leah was so starved for Jacob's attention that she hired him to her bed with mandrakes (Gen. 30:16). Mandrakes were considered an aphrodisiac: they were believed not only to excite love and sexual animation but also to produce conception. Here we see the superstitious side of Leah, who held on to vestiges of the pagan practice of her homeland—and not only her but also Jacob and Rachel. The latter was so desperate to conceive that she swallowed her pride and begged for Leah's mandrakes, believing they would help her to achieve her desire. What is startling though is that Rachel deferred to Leah's wishes to sleep with Jacob without putting up a fight. Mandrakes or no mandrakes, Jacob's heart was with Rachel, and she was certain about his desire for her. Nevertheless, her reaction had a note of resignation, as if to say, "Since you have mandrakes, let him sleep with you" because she said, "Therefore he shall lie with thee tonight for thy son's mandrakes" (Gen. 30:16 KJV).

Rachel's action reveals several things about her character. Her superstitious beliefs surpassed her longing for children because she strongly believed that the mandrakes could enhance sexual fervency and fertility. It appears that she had some affection for Leah although she was jealous of her sister's ability to bear children. Or perhaps she had some fear or respect for her since Leah was the older of the two.

The last thing is she knew her husband so well that she was almost sure he would succumb to Leah's plea to come to her bed because he too believed in the aphrodisiac quality of the mandrakes. Yes, he was a monotheistic believer of Yahweh and not one who practiced divination (unlike his father-in-law), but he was not completely rid of the superstitious beliefs of his Mesopotamian heritage. Jacob was a man still in the prime of his life, and if he was offered the opportunity of producing another son, he was going to take it, even if it meant deferring his sexual gratification with his beloved Rachel for a night with her more fertile sister. Despite the means that Leah used to draw Jacob to her bed, God intervened and she conceived Issachar. Subsequently she gave birth to Zebulun and a daughter called Dinah.

One may argue that regardless of Jacob's desire or lack of desire for Leah, it seems hardly unlikely that he would refuse to lie with her if she offered herself to him since she was the mother of most of his sons. However, the names of her children belie the fact that his visits to her bed were motivated by his interest in her as a woman and not mainly out of necessity. Her response to Rachel when the latter requested her mandrakes vividly shows the deep bitterness that Leah held against her sister for having Jacob's heart:

"And [Leah] said unto her, "Is it a small matter that thou hast taken my husband? and wouldest thou take away my son's mandrakes also?" (Gen. 30:15 KJV).

Such a scathing accusation against Rachel elicits our sympathy for her since she had to wait to be married after being ousted by her sister, although she was Jacob's first choice for a wife. The fact is that neither of the sisters were guilty of any wrongdoing with Jacob since all the circumstances pertaining to their marriages were arranged solely by their father, Laban. They were placed in a situation in which they had little or no control.

And who could harshly criticize Leah, a scorned wife? Why shouldn't she vent her frustration since her sister dared to try to rob her of an opportunity to invite her husband to her bed, even if she had to hire him with mandrakes? She was going to make Rachel experience guilt for being Jacob's favorite wife by accusing her of conning her son out of his mandrakes and stealing her husband. Sometimes revenge can be sweet even if the object of revenge is one's sister!

However, God will have mercy on whomever He will, and He opened Rachel's womb. She conceived and gave birth to Jacob's "long awaited love child," whom she named Joseph because she said God had taken away her reproach. Joseph's arrival marked a pivotal time in Jacob's life because it was after his birth that Jacob decided to leave Laban's home with his family and go to Canaan. With the new addition from Rachel to the family, Jacob saw the need to separate from his father-in-law, who had benefited from his services without compensating him for his work. Jacob would have taken his wives and children without requiring any of his wages due from Laban, but God blessed him immensely without any substantial help from his father-in-law.

Give me my inheritance

Even if some of his reasons for welcoming Jacob in his home were altruistic, Laban was shrewd enough to realize that he was a profitable addition. Laban, having found out that he would have jeopardized his own blessings, asked Jacob what he would require in exchange for the services he had already given. Jacob gave a simple request to have the brown animals among the sheep and the speckled and spotted animals among the cattle and goats. Ostensibly, Jacob's request was not only paltry but also silly in the eyes of any farmer. The reason was that the majority of Laban's flock was white if they were sheep, and brown or black if they were goats or cattle. Moreover, the brown sheep and speckled and spotted goats were considered an anomaly in the flock, so there were not enough of them to breed in order to become a substantial farmer.

Laban was confident that he had gotten the better end of the bargain. However, he was in for a rude awakening when he found out that Jacob not only had the better deal, but he also had it many times over. To make it even harder to swallow, Laban also realized that Jacob prospered not because he was shrewd but because he was divinely favored. As a matter of fact, he had heard the story about Abraham and how rich and influential he became after he left their country and turned wholly to serving Yahweh. How could Laban have forgotten that Abraham and his father, Bethuel, had pronounced blessings on Rebekah and her offspring before she left for Canaan to become Isaac's wife? He was present when Abraham's servant described for him the miraculous power of God in choosing Rebekah for Isaac (Genesis 24). Moreover, the marriage of his nephew to his two daughters also should have cemented the filial relationship between them. However, this did not prove to be true. Neither of them trusted each other, and there was good reason for each of them to be suspicious of the other: Laban could very likely have found out about Jacob's ploy against Esau, and Laban had reneged so many times on his word that Jacob had little or no reason to trust him.

Laban's ruthlessness became so pronounced after God caused Jacob's flocks to increase that it did not go unnoticed by Rachel and Leah. They had watched as their father extorted an excessive dowry from their husband as he worked relentlessly seven years for each of them. He also continued to work extra years without any compensation from Laban. Ten times their father had changed Jacob's wages and yet he tried to do right toward his father-in-law. The sisters were aware that God had intervened on Jacob's behalf because Laban had done evil toward him. Both sisters felt that their father had abandoned them through jealousy and deceit. Therefore, their response to Jacob's complaint about Laban's injustice toward him was not only their criticism of his greed, but it also was an indictment against his indifference toward their children's and his grandchildren's inheritance.

As was customary, Laban should have paid a dowry to Jacob before the marriage of each of his daughters (which he did not do). The dowry was the guaranteed support for the daughter and her family if her husband died or deserted her. Likewise, the groom was expected to pay a bride price to the family of his bride for the loss of their daughter. Jacob paid his bride price with laborious work for fourteen years. Not only did Leah and Rachel resent Laban for stealing their inheritance, but they also realized that the favor of God was toward Jacob; therefore, it was in their best interest to side with him.

The two sisters were used to the repeated accounts that Jacob told about the miraculous power of God in the lives of Isaac and Abraham, as well as his own encounter with the Creator. Laban was not oblivious to the story of divine intervention on Jacob's side of the family; he was present when Abraham's trusted servant came to seek a wife for Isaac and Laban gave his blessing for his sister Rebekah to be given in marriage to Isaac (Gen. 24:50–59). Therefore, it seemed strange to his daughters that their father did not act in a more upright manner toward his nephew and son-in-law, knowing that God had made a covenant with Jacob's grandfather, Abraham, and to his seed. They were convinced that the inheritance of their younger brothers would not be jeopardized if Jacob and his family were to be given their just reward by Laban.

May the gods avenge ...

According to *de jure* law, Laban's firstborn son should have had full primogeniture rights. Conversely, *de facto* action showed that Jacob was Laban's true heir, if not the legitimate one. Why? Because Laban had welcomed Jacob into his family as his first son, and Jacob had married his two daughters, was the father of his grandchildren, was the son of Laban's sister, and had worked for him for many years without wages, causing Laban to increase in wealth. The eldest son, along with all his benefits, received the family gods as part of his inheritance, thereby affirming his position as protector of the family. These gods were owned and worshipped by each family. They were believed to protect the affairs of that family and were sometimes consulted as oracles. Rachel, who clearly was aware of the significance of these gods, stole them from her home when Jacob fled Mesopotamia with his family.

Perhaps by taking the idols she was making a statement to her extended family that although Jacob was not a biological son of Laban, he was worthy of sonship because of his faithfulness, unrewarded service, and the undeserving benefits that her father reaped because Jacob was living in his house. Rachel was even more peeved after constantly hearing the unjustified complaints of her younger brothers, which they dared to make in earshot of Jacob. It was no secret that God was with Jacob and that Laban was blessed through Him, yet Laban did not try to dispel the complaints of his sons. Instead he exacerbated the situation by being sullen toward Jacob.

> And he heard the words of Laban's sons, saying, Jacob hath taken away all that was our father's; and of that which was our father's hath he gotten all this glory. (Gen. 31:1 KJV)

When Jacob was not out in the cold and heat taking care of Laban's sheep and other livestock, he mostly spent his time with Rachel. They must have talked about his encounter with God at Bethel and his other experiences. Therefore, she developed a relationship with Him that was closer than that of her sister or father. He was both lover and role model for her because she was passionately in love with him, and he with her. Moreover, she saw in him the integrity and faithfulness that she found lacking in her father. Although not a perfect man, Jacob had a strong faith in one God and believed that his life was ordered by Him. What a contrast to a father who depended on divination and put his trust in man-made idols!

Rachel had emotionally suffered in silence as her beloved worked fourteen years just to have her as his wife and additional years without any compensation from her unscrupulous father. She had dreamed of being in the arms of Jacob as soon as she found out that he had asked her father for her hand in marriage. Despite the emotional pain she felt thinking that Leah would feel the warmth of Jacob's embrace on what should have been her wedding night, Rachel later took comfort in the knowledge that he desired her so much that he would subject himself to another seven years of hard work for her. Although she was angry with her sister for being the first to marry Jacob, she also felt resentment toward her father for deceiving both her and her husband.

There was compatibility between her and Jacob from the first day they met at the well: the knitting of two hearts together. Nothing would diminish their love for each other—not the physical separation when Jacob was out in the cold caring for sheep, not the fruitfulness of Leah's womb, not the wickedness of Laban, nor even the childlessness of Rachel during most of her life with Jacob. The most poignant show of Jacob's deep love for Rachel was manifested when he placed her last at the meeting with his brother Esau after he fled from Paddan-Aram. Jacob was afraid for his life and the lives of his family before he met Esau for the first time after deceiving him and fleeing to Haran. Therefore, he decided to appease his brother by sending him gifts and introducing him to the members of his household in order of their importance to him. Consequently, he presented Leah and her children second to last, and finally Rachel and Joseph because of his great love for them.

> Now Jacob lifted his eyes and looked, and there, Esau was coming, and with him were four hundred men. So he divided the children among Leah, Rachel, and the two maidservants. And he put the maidservants and their children in front, Leah and her children behind, and Rachel and Joseph last. Then he crossed over before them and bowed himself to the ground seven times, until he came near to his brother. (Gen. 33:1–3 KJV)

Unfortunately, the love that held them together was the same thing that would separate them.

Rachel had taken her family's idols as a statement to Laban on Jacob's behalf (howbeit without Jacob's knowledge), but her action would be the cause of her untimely death. When Laban realized that his teraphim had been stolen, he was wrought and chased after Jacob when the latter fled Haran. He questioned Jacob about the idols. Jacob, not knowing that his Rachel had taken them, gave Laban permission to search his household and pronounced a curse of death on the person in whose possession they were found. Had he known that his beloved Rachel had the accursed idols, he would not have made such a declaration. However, like Achan, she would have to bear the consequences of her actions (Josh. 17). She was not stoned by her people, which was the fate of Achan and his family, but she died during childbirth and was buried along the way to Ephrath (Gen. 35:16–20).

Rachel was not laid to rest in the family plot with Jacob, Abraham and Sarah, and Isaac and Rebekah. Instead it was Leah, and not her sister, who was buried beside Jacob in the cave of Machpelah with his ancestors (Gen. 49:29–32). Abraham had bought the cave and field from Ephron the Hittite as a burial place for his family after the death of Sarah (Gen. 23). It was very important to Jacob that his body would be returned from Egypt after his death and buried in the same place as Abraham, Isaac, Sarah, Rebekah, and Leah—the wife whom he had spurned while Rachel was alive. In death he finally accorded to her the place she deserved as his first wife and the mother of his children. His charge to his sons regarding the interment of his body and his mention of Leah is evidence of the mighty power of God in the lives of his people. In it, Jacob named his predecessors and their wives, and he stated that they were buried in the cave of Machpelah, but he used the personal "I" to emphasize that he buried Leah there as an affirmation of her rightful position as his wife.

> And he charged them, and said unto them, I am to be gathered unto my people: bury me with my fathers in the cave that is in the field of Ephron the Hittite, In the cave that is in the field of Machpelah, which is before Mamre, in the land of Canaan, which Abraham bought with the field of Ephron the Hittite for a possession of a buryingplace. There they buried Abraham and

Sarah his wife; there they buried Isaac and Rebekah his wife; and there I buried Leah. (Gen. 49:29–32 KJV)

By his acknowledgment, that he had buried Leah in the family burial plot with his mother and grandmother, we get a glimpse of a man who has been changed by God's own hand. Here we see the amazing transformation of Jacob from the wily and guileful son of Rebekah to the righteous Israel, the sagacious head of his clan who was in tune with the God of Abraham and Isaac.

Although God did not deal with Jacob and his family with the same degree of severity that he meted out to Achan (Josh. 17), Jacob knew enough about Him to understand that He would not share His glory with any other gods. Therefore, after God commanded him to return to Bethel and prepare an altar to Him, Jacob instructed his house to remove all of the idols from among them:

And Jacob said to his household and to all who were with him, "Put away the foreign gods that are among you, purify yourselves, and change your garments. Then let us arise and go up to Bethel; and I will make an altar there to God, who answered me in the day of my distress and has been with me in the way which I have gone." So they gave Jacob all the foreign gods which were in their hands, and the earrings which were in their ears; and Jacob hid them under the terebinth tree which was by Shechem. (Gen. 35:2–4 KJV)

The children of Israel were to be a set-apart people whom God had chosen to be a light in the world and through whom all the peoples of the earth would be blessed. He would not tolerate any act or thing that would threaten His purpose for them. Although what Rachel did by bringing idols in the camp of Israel appeared to be an innocuous act, it violated the *a priori* basis for separation that is echoed in Deuteronomy 6:4: "Hear O Israel, the Lord our God, is one Lord." When God commanded Abraham to leave his people and go to a foreign land, he was basically telling Abraham to forsake his other gods and the gods of other nations, and pledge complete fidelity to him. As a reward for faithfulness, God would prosper and protect his people: those who blessed them would be blessed, and those who cursed them or did them harm would be cursed by Him.

All other nations would know that the Israelites were a chosen people because of the very fact that they served only one God. Therefore, Rachel's act was a covert threat to the survival of the Jewish people and an affront (even if a mild one) to whom God was to Abraham, Isaac, and Jacob. God clearly showed from the beginning of his call to Abraham and his interactions with Jacob that he would not share his glory with any other gods, person, or thing. They should not keep or serve idols, nor should they commingle with idolatrous nations. He continually reminded them of His requirement. If they disobeyed, there would always be a less or more severe consequence depending on their knowledge of His directives.

Rachel, was not ignorant of God's stance on idolatry, and regardless of her motive for bringing the idols on her journey to Canaan and her subsequent lying, she would be held responsible for her action. Not only did she defile herself and all the members of Jacob's household by bringing the idols into her tent, but she also covered her action by deceiving both her father and Jacob, whom she knew feared the Lord greatly. In order not to be searched by her father as he sought his idols, she convinced him that she could not get up from her saddle because she was having her monthly period (Gen. 31:34–35). Laban did not dare to challenge her because to do so would be utterly shameful and scandalous. However, because Rachel was not searched, the idols went undetected by Jacob and others, but not by God.

According to her custom, a menstruous woman was considered unclean and anyone who touched her or what she touched would also be considered unclean. It was ironic that Rachel would intimate that she would defile her father because of her physical condition, and not be aware that she was spiritually unclean because she made a conscious decision to perpetuate idolatry by taking her father's images from her homeland to the place God had chosen for his people. While she was in her father's house, although these idols were present, she was free from any blame regarding them. Unwittingly, by her own mouth, she deemed herself unclean.

Nevertheless, God was still gracious and allowed her to live to conceive the son that she predicted she would bear after Joseph, whose name means "May God grant me another son" (Gen. 30:22–24). However, the birth of her second child was bittersweet because she did not live to hold him in her arms or let him suck from her own breasts. As the midwife announced the birth of her baby boy in a frantic effort to comfort her, she gasped out, "Benoni" ("son of my trouble"). Her son, though not a comfort to her, was a comfort to his father in his old age: the first and only of his children born to him outside the household of Laban and after God changed his name to Israel (Gen. 35:10). Since God had reaffirmed the Abrahamic covenant with him, Jacob adopted a more confident view of life; therefore, he changed Benoni's name to Benjamin, which means "son of my right hand."

> And it came to pass, when [Rachel] was in hard labour, that the midwife said unto her, Fear not; thou shalt have this son also. And it came to pass, as her soul was in departing, (for she died) that she called his name Benoni: but his father called him Benjamin. (Gen. 35:16–20 NKJV)

In contrast to the popularity and favor that Rachel enjoyed during her youth, her adult years were filled with sorrow and bitterness because of her barrenness. Although she had Jacob's love, it could not suffice for her yearning to bear children. She spent a considerable part of her married life dogged by jealousy of her more fruitful sister, Leah. God eventually granted her request, but her joy was short-lived because she did not have a long time to savor her victory. She was blessed to see some of Joseph's formative years and perhaps only caught an agonizing glimpse of Benjamin through her pain-drenched eyes. Her death was a haunting reminder of the curse that Eve brought on all women because of her sin of disobedience: the agony of childbirth. What a tragic picture of joy and sorrow in one short-lived life!

No wonder Rachel is the iconic matriarch of Israel (and not Leah, though mother of most of Jacob's sons). She is mentioned in both Jeremiah 31:15 and Matthew 2:18 as the mother who wept for her dead children and could not be comforted. Jeremiah's prophecy is twofold. It speaks of the unimaginable grief that would result from the impending Babylonian conquest of Judah and also foretells the massacre of Jewish male children under two years of age that would be sanctioned by Herod the Great after the birth of Christ. He would order the execution to ensure that no male baby would later have ascendancy to the Jewish throne after hearing from the wise men that the Jewish promised Messiah was born. Matthew pointed his Jewish readers to the Old Testament by reminding them of Jeremiah's prophecy, which was fulfilled after Jesus was born, to convince them that Jesus was the true Messiah. He presented the prophecy in Matthew 2 (KJV) as it was written in Jeremiah 31:15 (KJV):

> A voice was heard in Ramah,
> Lamentation and bitter weeping,
> Rachel weeping for her children,
> Refusing to be comforted for her children,
> Because they are no more.

Jeremiah succinctly captured the agony and overwhelming grief of Jewish mothers in portraying Rachel as the maternal symbol of Israel. Matthew also left little room for his scripturally discriminating Jewish readers to argue the authenticity of Christ by drawing on Jeremiah's prophecy with its allusion to Rachel, who is highly regarded and endeared in Jewish tradition. Ramah is used here figuratively as the scene of Rachel's weeping because it represents Israel (twelve tribes, not only Judah). Ramah is also significant because it was part of the allotment given to Benjamin (Joshua 18:25) and the place this tribe returned to after their captivity (Ezra 2:26). It would not be extremely hard for an open-minded Jew to make the connection with Rachel and the circumstances that coincided with the birth of Christ.

In Micah 5:2 (KJV) the prophecy of the place of Christ's birth pointed to Bethlehem, which is also Ephrath, the place on the way to where Rachel was buried:

> But you, Bethlehem Ephrathah,
> Though you are little among the thousands of Judah,
> Yet out of you shall come forth to Me
> The One to be Ruler in Israel,
> Whose goings forth are from of old,
> From everlasting.

We know the truth that Jesus was born in the Bethlehem of Judah and that he brought rest to Israel and the whole world, although many still do not recognize it because it was a spiritual rest and not as the Israelites had imagined it. In a similar manner, Rachel's impact may also be overlooked in her contribution to the formation of the Israelite nation because her story is marred by her jealousy of her sister, her struggle to conceive children, and the idolatry that ultimately cost her, her life.

Her greatest triumph is in the story of her first son, Joseph, who, though not the person from whose tribe the Messiah came, was the recipient of his father's birthright and was one of the most powerful men in one of the greatest empires in history (Gen. 41:38–52). Jacob predicted that Judah would receive homage from his brethren (Gen. 49:8–10), but that Joseph would be "a fruitful bough, even a fruitful bough by a well; whose branches run over the wall" (Gen. 49:22 KJV) because he had boundless blessings. God chose Joseph as the one among Jacob's eleven sons to preserve the children of Israel during their harsh years of famine, and He provided a haven for them in the land of Egypt. Joseph inherited his mother's stoic reserve and clung to his father's deep faith in God that helped him to survive in dire circumstances in a strange land. Though he suffered deeply by the hands of his brothers and cousins, he learned to forgive—in many ways he was a typology of our suffering Savior who would cry out on the cross, "Father, forgive them. For they know not what they do" (Luke 23:34 KJV). Centuries before the advent of Christ, Joseph had shown mercy to his jealous brothers when they were terribly afraid that he would avenge them for the great harm they had done to him.

> Joseph said to them, "Do not be afraid, for am I in the place of God? But as for you, you meant evil against me; but God meant it for good, in order to bring it about as it is this day, to save many people alive. Now therefore, do not be afraid; I will nourish you and your little ones." And he comforted them and spake kindly unto them. (Gen. 50:19–21 KJV)

His words to them are what Christianity is about: grace and forgiveness. They show us that the crucifixion of Christ was Satan's intent to destroy God's kingdom, but it worked as God intended for the redemption of all humankind.

CHAPTER 6

A Seal, A Cord, and A Staff

I looked down through the lattice.
I saw among the simple,
I noticed among the young men,
,a youth who had no sense.
(Prov. 7:6–7 NIV)

Then out came a woman to meet him,
dressed like a prostitute and with crafty intent.
(Prov. 7:10 NIV)

The book of Proverbs delves into human issues and foibles like no other book in the Bible, and it has stood the test of time because it strikes a pragmatic stance without sacrificing its godly purpose. Chapter 6 of this book bears some resemblance to the scenario played out in Genesis 38, though not completely. Tamar, who is the protagonist in Genesis 38, was not an adulteress or a true prostitute, but rather she was a virtuous wife determined to preserve the name and lineage of her deceased husband. Judah was not a hapless youth but a father of grown sons. What is true in both scenarios is that a prostitute enticed an unsuspecting paramour to her bed.

The unsuspecting lover in Genesis is Judah, a man in his prime and also past his prime, though not an old man. He was the fourth son of Leah and Jacob, and appears to have left the confines of his father's estate to seek other diversions besides rearing sheep. He found a Canaanite wife (a marriage most likely not approved by his mother and father), and she bore him three sons: Er, Onan, and Shelah. When his first son came of age, he also found him a Canaanite maiden, and there began the saga of Tamar and Judah.

Judah is mentioned for the first time in Genesis 29 at his birth by the name his mother gave him, which means "This time I will praise the Lord." Nothing is said about him until chapter 37 where he convinced his other brothers not to kill Joseph, but rather sell him as a slave to Ishmaelite traders on their way to Egypt who subsequently sold him to Potiphar, an officer of Pharaoh and captain of the guard (Gen. 37:26–38). Judah turns up in chapter 38 but not in a positive light. The Bible states, "At that time, Judah left his brothers and went down to stay with a man of Adullam named Hirah" (Gen. 38:1). It was at the time when Judah was away from the watchful eyes of his father and brethren that his darker side was revealed in his relationship with his sons and his interactions with his daughter-in-law. Being out of sight and probably out of mind by his extended family members, Judah had married a Canaanite woman, knowing that his grandfather had made it clear to his father, Jacob, that he should not marry a Canaanite woman but take one from among his own people (Gen. 28:1). His great-grandfather Abraham had even been more emphatic by having his trusted servant swear that he would not get a wife for Isaac from the "daughters of the Canaanites."

> And Abraham was old and well stricken in age: and the Lord had blessed Abraham in all things. And Abraham said unto his eldest servant of his house, that ruled over all that he had, Put, I pray thee, thy hand under my thigh: And I will make thee swear by the Lord, the God of heaven, and the God of the earth, that thou shalt not take a wife unto my son of the daughters of the Canaanites, among whom I dwell: But thou shalt go unto my

country, and to my kindred, and take a wife unto my son Isaac. (Gen. 24:1–4 KJV)

However, he disregarded the desires of his predecessors and not only married a daughter of the Canaanites, but he also chose Tamar, the wife for his eldest son, from among them. Unfortunately, his son Er died and Tamar became a widow. God killed him because he was wicked. Judah's second son, Onan, was therefore obligated under Levirate law to marry Er's widow, who died childless, in order to preserve Er's name and produce heirs for his estate. Onan grudgingly married Tamar merely to obey the law, but he deliberately practiced coitus interruptus or spilled his semen on the ground so he would not impregnate her and raise children for his deceased brother. God became displeased with him and killed him for his selfishness. Judah, fearing that his youngest son, Shelah, would also be killed, encouraged Tamar to return to her parents' home to live as a widow, promising to give his son in marriage to her as soon as he was of age. However, Judah reneged on his word and did not give his son in marriage to her as he promised although Shelah was then a grown man.

Tamar, being a wise woman and desiring to honor her husband's memory, decided to force Judah's hand in complying with the Levirate custom. Her chance came after Judah's wife died and he had completed his time of mourning. After fulfilling the customary time of mourning for his deceased wife, Judah was ready to get back to his normal lifestyle. Therefore, accompanied by his friend, he decided to go up to Timnah and visit the men who were hired to shear his sheep. Tamar received news that he was on his way there, so she disguised herself as a prostitute to entice him to sleep with her. Judah passed along the route where she was lying in wait for him and was seduced by her. As compensation for her services, Judah promised her a goat from his flock, and in turn she requested his staff, cord, and seal as a pledge that he would honor his word.

Three months later, after trying to find the "harlot," pay her, and retrieve his valuables from her, he found out that Tamar was pregnant. He became angry because he heard that her pregnancy was the result of her harlotry and desired that she be burned to death. What a rude awakening he had when he learned that he was the one who should have been punished for his sin toward her! His staff, cord, and seal were exhibits of his dishonesty. His head must have hung very low when she returned them to him. He realized to his own shame that he would be father and grandfather to his son's seed because he had dealt dishonorably with his widow. He had flouted his own conventions by not upholding the Levirate law and not keeping his word to his daughter-in-law. Nevertheless, Judah redeemed himself by accepting his wrongdoing and refrained from having subsequent sexual interactions with her: Judah said, "She hath been more righteous than I; because that I gave her not to Shelah my son. And he knew her again no more" (Gen. 38:26 KJV).

Despite the unseemly act of both Tamar and Judah, God did not leave Judah without grandchildren. In order to fulfill the covenant that he had given to Abraham, God allowed Tamar to bear twins that would be seed for her deceased husband and for Judah. Their birth bears an uncanny resemblance to that of Esau and Jacob. Zerah and Perez (Tamar's twins), like Esau and Jacob, engaged in unusual activities at birth. The Bible states that Esau and Jacob jostled in their mother's womb and that Jacob grabbed the heel of Esau as his brother preceded him during birth. While there is no record of Perez's and his brother's activity in the womb, we are told that at birth Zerah pushed out his hand and was tagged by the midwife with a scarlet thread, and as he withdrew it into the warmth of his mother's uterus, his brother Perez broke forth from the confines of the womb and preempted him in birth:

> And it came to pass in the time of her travail, that, behold, twins were in her womb. And it came to pass, when she travailed, that the one put out his hand: and the midwife took and bound upon his hand a scarlet thread, saying, This came out first.

> And it came to pass, as he drew back his hand, that, behold, his brother came out: and she said, How hast thou broken forth? this breach be upon thee: therefore his name was called Pharez. And afterward came out his brother, that had the scarlet thread upon his hand: and his name was called Zarah. (Gen. 38:27–30 KJV)

Perez, the younger, would be the one through whose lineage Christ would originate, and not from his brother, Zerah, who should have been the first to come from his mother's womb. Jacob, the younger of Rebekah's twins, had stolen the birthright from Esau and become the predecessor of both Zerah and Perez.

Let there be praise ...

From the mention of his birth, his complicity in the selling of his half-brother Joseph, and up to the point of his marriage, his widowhood, and his sexual encounter with Tamar in Genesis 38, much of what has been said about Judah does not bear the stamp of a good character reference. Apparently, he was not the most righteous of his father's children, nor was he the eldest. He also inherited some of Jacob's past proclivity for artifice and his grandfather Laban's knack for unfairness and trickery. Yet he was chosen to be the leader among all his brothers and an ancestor of Jesus Christ. What he possessed was the grace of God and the blessing of his father, Jacob. He had sold his brother Joseph to Ishmaelite traders for twenty pieces of silver and lied to his father to make him believe that a wild animal killed Joseph. He also committed sexual immorality with Tamar. However, all the things that he did wrong appear to be less than the things that he did right.

Although he was a participant in the selling of Joseph, Judah was also instrumental in convincing his brothers not to harm him. He was the one who encouraged Jacob to send Benjamin with his other brothers to Egypt, as Joseph commanded, and he offered himself as a surety for the young man's life. Judah also mustered up the courage to speak to Joseph and asked to be held as a slave in Egypt in place of Benjamin to protect his brother from possible harm and his father from grief, knowing that being second only to the pharaoh, Joseph could have imprisoned or killed him (Gen. 44:18–34). Judah was the son whom Jacob trusted to go ahead of him to Egypt in order to make the necessary arrangements and work out the logistics for his arrival in the Goshen (Gen. 46:28). At this point in his life, Jacob must have seen the beginning of the leadership role that Judah would play in the future. Reuben had already forfeited his position as head of his brethren because of his dastardly act of sleeping with his father's concubine. Levi and Simeon were rejected for the murders they had committed. In his final blessing to Judah, Jacob would declare that the man who was a liar, a deceiver, and a co-conspirator in a plot to banish his own brother would receive obeisance and homage from his brethren:

"The scepter would not depart from him, Nor a lawgiver from between his feet, Until Shiloh comes; And to Him shall the gathering of the people be" (Gen. 49:10 KJV).

This prophecy speaks of the specific blessing of Judah whose position was elevated among his own brothers and the people of Israel, but it also predicts the coming of Jesus Christ, who would bring redemption for all peoples. Here, Shiloh is seen both as Christ the Redeemer and the redemptive act that would occur as a result of his incarnation. The Redeemer would fulfill the twofold role of king and lawgiver—one equipped to be sovereign and judge. Jacob's pronouncement on his deathbed to Judah was like the prelude to what David would prophesy for many generations: that one of his descendants would always sit on his throne. Psalm 132:11 and 2 Samuel 7:12–16 substantiate that David, also Judah's descendant and an ancestor of Jesus, would have an everlasting throne. Considering that David is dead, the longevity could only be fulfilled through Jesus who is alive for evermore and whose kingdom is eternal. Likewise, Jacob predicted that Judah would receive praise and triumph over his enemies, yet Judah was not a king or a ruler in his lifetime. Again, the prophecy points to Christ, who has vanquished sin and will completely annihilate Satan and his hosts when he returns to the earth. The name of Judah is also used here as a metonymy for the tribe that would spring from the fourth son of Jacob and Leah.

> Judah, you are he whom your brothers shall praise;
> Your hand shall be in the neck of your enemies;
> Your father's children shall bow down before thee.
> (Gen. 49:8 KJV)

God would not treat Judah according to his sins, and giving him an honored position among his brethren is one of the many outpourings of grace that we have received through Christ's death.

On the other hand, Mary's genealogical ties are not directly stated as in the case of Joseph, though there is evidence to support the claim that she too was connected to the Davidic line of Christ. Some scholars assert that Luke 2:23–38 supports the validity of this claim though others disagree—and for obvious reasons. One of the main points of the opposing camp is that there is no clear statement that Mary was a descendant of King David in either of the two Gospels, and there are several differences in the names of the ancestors in the two accounts. Luke 3:23 describes Joseph as "the son of Heli," and in Matthew 1:16, his paternity is given to Jacob, the father of Joseph, "the husband of Mary, of whom was born Jesus, who is called Christ." The facts are undeniable: it would be biologically impossible for Joseph, who was not man and not God (as Jesus is), to have had two fathers; therefore, there must be a plausible explanation for these two differing accounts and the answer is rooted in the word of God.

"Wherefore when he cometh into the world, he saith, Sacrifice and offering thou wouldest not, but a body hast thou prepared me" (Heb. 10:5 KJV).

In general, many Bible scholars use a humanistic construct to interpret the Bible. Often when they cannot explain certain phenomena in "logical" terms, they feel obligated to frame it in a certain schema to make it comprehensible to the natural individual. It is understandable because we are natural beings, and without the enlightenment of the One who designed our blueprint, we are restricted in what we can perceive. Notwithstanding, the Bible is able to answer the questions it poses and bring clarity to its apparent contradictions. We must never forget that it is the inspired word of God and not a collection of "cunningly devised fables" (2 Pet. 1:16). nor that any "prophecy of the scripture is of any private interpretation" (2 Pet. 1:20). It would be unlikely and out of character for Luke, who was meticulous in his records and so desired to bring awareness to those who had little or no knowledge of the intertestamental connection of the holy scriptures, and also Matthew, who wrote to a theologically discriminating audience, to have made such obvious errors about the bedrock of Christianity—the incarnation of Christ.

Peter tells us clearly in 2 Peter 1:19–21 that the word did not come by the will of man but by the will of God, and in 2 Timothy 3:16, we learn that it is for instruction, correction, and illumination. It is "like silver tried in a furnace of the earth, purified seven times "(Psalm 12:6) and stands the test of time as the perfect guide for righteous living. Therefore, there is a strong reason to believe that the genealogical record of Christ in Luke's naming Joseph as the son of Heli and Matthew's naming Jacob as his father is not an error. Additionally, the only two names in both genealogies, besides Joseph, that match are Zorobabel and Salathiel. However, there is no clear evidence that they are the same people in both genealogies. This leads us to conclude that since both family trees are so obviously different, both writers were tracing Christ's lineage through two different people.

The reason for the differences is without question if we understand that each book was written for a different purpose, and although the content of each book transcends the scope of the writers' physical sphere, it was also pertinent to the cultural context in which the author was writing. Matthew's Gospel was written to Jews who were already familiar with the Old Testament books and had to be convinced of the royal lineage of Christ through King David. Unlike Luke, Matthew skipped the preface to his first chapter and immediately delved into the genealogy of Christ starting with Abraham because every Jewish person accepts him as the principal patriarch of their nation. It was also common knowledge that the promised Messiah would come from the line of King David; therefore, Matthew wasted no time in giving superfluous information, having only to establish Jesus's ties to the Davidic throne. Having done so, he would also prove without question that Christ was the seed of Abraham through Joseph. Hence he began the Gospel: "The book of the genealogy of Jesus Christ, the Son of David, the Son of Abraham"(Matt. 1:1). He traced the line from Abraham to David; mentioned Solomon, who was next in the royal line to his father, David; to Joseph; and then to Jesus, the legal heir to the throne of David.

In contrast, Luke traced Christ's Davidic lineage through Nathan, a lesser-known son. Luke used Nathan as a marker here not to try to establish Christ's royal heritage, but to emphasize the dichotomous human and spiritual essence of Jesus Christ. Note that he encapsulated his genealogical account starting with Jesus and ending with Adam and then God (Luke 3:23–38). He wanted to prove that Jesus was fully man and fully God: though being a partaker of human experiences remained not aloof, but above the baseness of sin that had separated us from our pristine existence before the Fall in the garden of Eden. Had Christ not been man, He would not have had the legal right to challenge Satan on behalf of humankind (though He had the power), and had He not been God, He would not have been a pure sacrifice that would be worthy to appease his Father, from whom He was begotten before the world was created. Christ was aware that the time was ordained when He would break into humanity and deliver the people from the evil one; therefore, when the time came, a body already had been prepared to receive him in the person of the Virgin Mary (Heb. 10:5). His God form was also transformed to conform to the restrictions of human existence in order to fulfill the will of His Father.

The Davidic Covenant

God had told [Satan] the serpent in the garden that his head would be bruised by the seed of the woman, and he would put enmity between his seed and her seed. Since Joseph was not the biological father of Jesus, His humanity would have to be established with His mother. It is important to note that God did not tell the serpent that Adam's seed would hurt him but that the seed of the woman would crush his head. It was from the breast of Mary that the Savior sucked and from her placenta that he was nourished; from her womb would emerge the man who would destroy the shackles of sin that held the human race captive, and also in her would the prophecy of David be fulfilled. In order to further substantiate that Christ was not just a legal heir of David through adoption by Joseph, we must also consider the natural line that came through Mary, having been the fruit of David's body and Jesus being the fruit of her body. It is impossible for God to lie, and He was clear about what He told David: the successor who would perpetuate His throne would be His natural descendant.

"The Lord hath sworn in truth unto David; he will not turn from it; Of the fruit of thy body will I set upon thy throne" (Ps. 132:11 KJV).

Luke wrote an account of Peter's speech on the day of Pentecost in which he alluded to David's prophecy in Psalm 132:11, which verifies that Jesus could have only been David's "bodily fruit" through Mary:

> Therefore being a prophet, and knowing that God had sworn with an oath to him, that of the fruit of his loins, according to the flesh, he would raise up Christ to sit on his throne. (Acts 2:30 KJV)

A parallel may be found in Genesis in the story of Isaac and Ishmael. God not only told Abraham that the son in whom his seed would be blessed would come from his loins but also that it would be from Sarah's womb. Abraham preempted God and begat Ishmael by his bondservant, but God told him that he was not the chosen son and agreed with Sarah that he be sent away. God showed His power by allowing Sarah to conceive when she was of a ripe old age and also fulfilled His promise to Abraham. In the same way, God fulfilled His promise to David in the person of Mary, who was the human receptacle for the Word that would be presented to humankind in due time. Several scriptures underscore how God would perform his word:

> And David my servant shall be king over them; and they all shall have one shepherd: they shall also walk in my judgments, and observe my statutes, and do them. And they shall dwell in the land that I have given unto Jacob my servant, wherein your fathers have dwelt; and they shall dwell therein, even they, and their children, and their children's children for ever: and my servant David shall be their prince for ever. (Ezek. 37:24–25 KJV)

> Of the increase of His government and peace
> There will be no end,
> Upon the throne of David and over His kingdom,
> To order it and establish it with judgment and justice
> From henceforth, even forever.
> The zeal of the Lord of hosts will perform this.
> (Isa. 9:7 KJV)

> Behold, the days come, saith the Lord, that I will raise unto David a righteous Branch, and a King shall reign and prosper, and shall execute judgment and justice in the earth. (Jer. 23:5 KJV)

> Behold, the days come, saith the Lord, that I will perform that good thing which I have promised unto the house of Israel and to the house of Judah. In those days, and at that time, will I cause the Branch of righteousness to grow up unto David; and he shall execute judgment and righteousness in the land. (Jer. 33:14–15 KJV)

The above scriptures are a testament to the fact that God is not slack concerning His promises and that He will perform what He has spoken. He had protected the seed in earthen vessels from Eve through Mary until it was time for the seed (Jesus Christ) to break into history. Although Mary did not remain a virgin throughout her lifetime (she bore other children with Joseph), it is significant to note that she was a virgin when she conceived and that "[Joseph] did not know her till she had brought forth her firstborn Son. And he called His name Jesus" (Matt. 1:25). She posed a question to the angel Gabriel during the Annunciation of her conception that would dispel any doubts that she was not a virgin, "How can this be, seeing, I know not a man?" It had to be very clear at this point that the conception of Jesus would have to be without human intervention and it must be known that the child was not the offspring of an earthly father. The angel's response to Mary was very specific about how conception would occur:

> And the angel answered and said unto her, The Holy Ghost shall come upon thee, and the power of the Highest shall overshadow thee: therefore also that holy thing which shall be born of thee shall be called the Son of God (Luke 1:35 KJV)

In other words, the angel was informing her that the act that would follow his announcement would be executed entirely by divine instrumentation and not subject to human interference. God nullified the Jewish conventions without negating the basic principles: He allowed a virgin to conceive without male insemination or the joining of an egg or a sperm, and at the same time, he provided an earthly father who would ensure that the child would be legitimate.

Mary could have been a single mother and remained a virgin, but that would have gone against the institution that God had established for the nurturing and care of children. It was already settled in heaven that she would be the mother of the Messiah; therefore, her acceptance of the angel's declaration, "Behold the maidservant of the Lord! Let it be to me according to your word," was an affirmation that she was a willing vessel. As we already know, the earthly descendants of David did not always obey God, so the royal line of David was destroyed. However, God kept his seed intact through the legal right of sonship, through Solomon, through Joseph, and his natural line through Nathan through Mary. Both of Christ's earthly parents were descendants of David, a fact that leaves no doubt about the veracity of the prophecies that the Messiah would come from the Davidic line.

Consequently, Luke's genealogical account of Christ does not contradict that of Matthew's but shows that both writers agree that the incarnation of Jesus converged in the person of King David, who was both the seed of Judah and Adam. Luke mentioned Joseph as the husband of Mary in his Gospel to make us aware that recognition of his inclusion in Christ's maternal lineage did not mitigate the value of Joseph's role as the head of his wife and paternal authority over his family:

> And in the sixth month the angel Gabriel was sent from God unto a city of Galilee, named Nazareth, to a virgin espoused to a man whose name was Joseph, of the house of David; and the virgin's name was Mary. (Luke 1:26–27 KJV)

> And Joseph also went up from Galilee, out of the city of Nazareth, into Judaea, unto the city of David, which is called Bethlehem; (because he was of the house and lineage of David:)

To be taxed with Mary his espoused wife, being great with child. (Luke 2:4–5 KJV)

The Son of ...

The names Son of man and Son of God, by which our Lord is referred to in the Bible, attest to the fact that He shares our humanity, while He remains head of all creation (Col. 1:15–20). Not only did the Jews refer to male descendants as sons of their predecessors, but Christ also refers to Himself as Son of man several times in the scriptures.[1]. We should also remember that *son* in the Bible is not always used literally and may refer to father/son ties, grandfather/grandson ties (regardless of generational differences), and even father-in-law/son ties.. The connection between adopted father and son and even uncle/son are also part of the paternal continuum. Since *son* can be interpreted in various ways, it makes sense to believe that "son of Heli" in Luke could also be interpreted as son-in-law through Joseph's adoption into Mary's family through marriage since it was apparent that her father had no male heirs and the names of women were not usually included in genealogical records.

Adoption of a son through marriage was permissible in Jewish society. It can be traced back to the law given by Moses in Numbers 1–11 after consulting God when the daughters of Zelophedad appealed to him regarding their lack of inheritance, and in Joshua 17:3–6 where the law was enforced. Women were not allowed to share in their father's inheritance in the nascent Jewish nation until Moses declared God had decreed that daughters had the right to an inheritance if their father died without sons. The law (Num. 36:1–11) was extended to restrict daughters who inherited their father's estate from marrying outside of their clan in order that their inheritance would not be added to another tribe.

---

[1]. See Daniel 7:13–14; Matthew 8:20; Luke 9:58; John 6:53, 63, 58; and Matthew 20:28.

In the same way that the scriptures point to Mary in the Old Testament without a direct mention of her name, Luke's genealogical table presents her ancestral ties to Jesus without directly stating her name. In Genesis 3:15, God pronounced judgment on the serpent through the victory of the woman's seed who achieves final victory. Contextually, "woman" refers to Eve and her descendants, although in a broader sense it refers to Mary, the then future mother of Jesus, and her seed. There is no mention of a man here or in preceding prophecies about the Messianic birth. Isaiah tells King Ahaz that God would deliver him from his enemies of Israel and Syria, and as a sign that His word would be fulfilled, the virgin would conceive and give birth to a Son:

> "Therefore the Lord Himself will give you a sign: Behold, the virgin shall conceive and bear a Son, and shall call His name Immanuel" (Isa. 7:14 KJV).

Typically, in the Bible, the announcement of a conception and birth of a child is first made to the father and not to the mother. In Genesis 15:17–19, the angel told Abraham that his wife would conceive and bear a son in her old age. The angel Gabriel announced to Zacharias, and not to his wife, Elizabeth, that she would also bear a son and his name would be John (Luke 1:13). However, the angel Gabriel first declared Mary's miraculous conception to her and proclaimed that his name would be Jesus: "And behold, you will conceive in your womb and bring forth a Son, and shall call His name Jesus" (Luke 1:31 KJV). Hannah, the mother of Samuel, conceived after she had prayed that God would remove her barrenness and Eli, the priest, blessed her (1 Samuel 1:1–20 KJV). Eli did not tell her that she would become pregnant but that God would grant her petition (1 Samuel 1:17). Hannah even named her son Samuel, she said, "because I have asked him of the Lord God" (1 Sam.1:20).

However, in Mary's case, she did not make any petition for a son—God initiated the act of conception through the power of the Holy Spirit. She accepted what God had chosen for her and presented her body as a living sacrifice to house the eternal Lord. It is extremely remarkable, if not incredulous, that a teenage girl engaged to be married did not become alarmed or anxious about how her fiancé would respond after finding out that she was carrying the child of another "man." If she did consider how she would break the news of her supernatural conception, she never voiced it to the angel. Her only concern was to find out how her pregnancy would occur, considering that she was chaste and that she and Joseph would not consummate their betrothal until the nuptial rites were complete. Hence the question, "How can this thing be seeing I know not a man?"

No wonder Mary was chosen from among all the women of the world. She was totally obedient to the will of God, not even perturbed that she would have to face Joseph, her parents, and the community to try to convince them about her purity. How different her response was from that of Zechariah, who was skeptical of the angel Gabriel's word to him about his impregnation of Elizabeth and the birth of their son (Luke 1:11–18). Zechariah was a priest who ministered in the temple and should have been aware of the power of God; therefore, he was struck with dumbness until the word of the angel had been fulfilled after his son John was born. Mary had been "carefully and wonderfully made" for the time of her visitation for the Son of God. The Psalmist David uttered these words (Ps. 139:14) regarding God's magnificent work in the creation of humankind, but they aptly describe the Virgin Mary's preparation to be the mother of Jesus. Isaiah 7:14 substantiates her purpose: "Therefore the Lord Himself will give you a sign: 'Behold, the virgin shall conceive and bear a Son, and shall call His name Immanuel.'" She would be a chaste young woman who would be "highly favored" (Luke 1:28). The definite article "the" in front of the word *virgin* gives specificity to the woman who would bear and give birth to Immanuel. "God is with us."

Highly favored

All the women recorded in the Bible who are in Christ's lineage (other women were part of his bloodline but not mentioned in the Bible), except Mary, had glaring fatal flaws that should have excluded them from the genealogy of the sinless Lamb—Tamar, Rahab, and Bathsheba being chief among them. Rahab was a harlot by profession; Tamar, a seductress and one-time prostitute; and Bathsheba, an adulteress. Nevertheless, God chose them to show His grace and mercy as a foreshadowing of the consummate grace that we would experience with the coming of His Son in "[whom] dwells all the fullness of the Godhead bodily; and [we] are complete in Him, who is the head of all principality and power" (Col. 2:9–10 KJV).

In comparison to the women named above and their less-than-wholesome pasts, Mary appeared to be without flaw. In some respect she was because she was a devout Jew as revealed in her response to Gabriel's news to her and her praise in the Magnificat. Moreover, she remained a virgin from the time of her conception until after the birth of Jesus because Joseph had no sexual interaction with her before or during the time of her pregnancy. She is a representation of the Church that will be without spot or wrinkle that Christ will receive when he returns. The Church is currently comprised of those who have accepted Jesus, have been cleansed by His blood, and have already become part of the "cloud of witnesses" that are no longer on earth, while others who are still alive are on earth waiting for their final redemption. Despite the sins that the Church has committed because of its redemption by the blood of Jesus, it will be made perfect for His coming. Each woman recorded in Christ's lineage before the time of Mary committed errors or were participants in acts that were not honorable, yet they were not rejected. When Mary arrived on the scene, she was without the "baggage" that some of her female ancestors had had and therefore was fit to accommodate the Word that was made flesh:

"And the Word became flesh and dwelt among us, (and we beheld His glory, the glory as of the only begotten of the Father), full of grace and truth" (John 1:14 KJV).

In the same way that Christ has been perfecting the Church since His first coming for the completion of its redemption in the second coming, God used various women, such as Sarah, Rahab, and Ruth in preparation for the Messianic birth that would culminate in the divine impregnation of the Virgin Mary. However, she was not sinless; neither was she divine, as some may believe. Had she been divine, Jesus would have not have been "firstborn over all creation" (Col. 1:15) and the "firstborn from among the dead, so that in everything he might have the supremacy" (Col. 1:18), or have legitimate right to subdue Satan on earth. The man who would defeat Satan would have to be born of a woman and also be God that through him all things could be reconciled once and for all in heaven and on earth. of sin Adam was not the firstborn man because he was created as an adult. He also disobeyed God and therefore was not qualified to save himself nor his descendants from the ravages of sin. Jesus Christ was the only one who had all the credentials to restore humanity to its former position since He was not a created being. He was the sinless begotten Son of God the Father and the seed of woman.

Jacob prophesied Christ's victory over the nations long before Jesus was born. He blessed Judah as the one through whom this would be accomplished, knowing that it would occur with his seed. The seed was in the loins of Judah to be preserved for the next generation. God could have chosen other sons and daughters besides Judah and Tamar to be the ancestors of Jesus, but again He chose the most unlikely candidates because He wanted to express His glory in vessels of clay.

CHAPTER 7

Ruth

Thy people shall be my people …

Not many daughters-in-law will share their homes with their mothers-in-law. Some wives will do everything in their power to avoid having interactions with them. The story of Ruth is a far cry from this norm. Its main focus is the great love of Ruth for her mother-in-law and how this love changed her life and ultimately placed her in Christ's family tree.

The story of Ruth takes place during the time when pre-monarchical Israel was comprised of a number of tribes led by various judges. Each tribe was joined together with the others by their common worship of Yahweh. Ruth 1:1 (KJV) confirms its historical setting:

> Now it came to pass in the days when the judges ruled, that there was a famine in the land. And a certain man of Bethlehem Judah went to sojourn in the country of Moab, he, and his wife, and his two sons.

Its physical setting begins in Bethlehem, Judah, or the southern part of Canaan; then Moab; and then back in Bethlehem. The book, which also bears the name of the principal character, tells about Naomi and Elimelech, a Jewish couple who left the land of Israel and went to find greener pastures in the land of Moab. They settled in Moab and appeared to have had initial success while raising two sons.

Unfortunately, Elimelech and his two sons died, leaving three widows: Naomi, Orpah, and Ruth. Naomi, having no way of surviving in her adopted country without her sons and husband, returned to her homeland. She entreated her two widowed daughters-in-law to remain in their country, but they insisted on accompanying her to Bethlehem. She eventually convinced Orpah to remain in Moab, but Ruth would not relent. Naomi, realizing that Ruth would not listen to her admonitions, gave in to her desire and brought her to the land that she and her family initially were forced to leave because of famine.

The arrival of Naomi and Ruth in Judah marks the true beginning of the life of Ruth and restoration of Naomi's faith in the God of Israel. The attitudes of the two women juxtaposed together before they left Moab are almost in stark contrast to each other. Naomi was bitter, complaining, and hopeless, while Ruth remained stoically patient, confident, and calm. Take note of what appears to be the pragmatic advice of Naomi, but when closely examined from a spiritual perspective, its foundation is specious. She speaks to her daughters-in-law like someone who has not been acquainted with Jehovah or even heard of his miraculous works in the lives of the children of Israel. Now look at Naomi's sense of bitterness, hopelessness, and complaint against God as she tries to convince both Ruth and Orpah to remain in Moab:

And Naomi said,

Turn again, my daughters: why will ye go with me? are there yet any more sons in my womb, that they may be your husbands? Turn again, my daughters, go your way; for I am too old to have an husband. If I should say, I have hope, if I should have an husband also to night, and should also bear sons; Would ye tarry for them till they were grown? would ye stay for them from

> having husbands? nay, my daughters; for it grieveth me much
> for your sakes that the hand of the Lord is gone out against me.
> (Ruth 1:11–13 KJV)

Fortunately, the complaints of Naomi do not overshadow the beginning
of the story because the admirable fortitude of Ruth serves as the perfect
foil for the hapless prating of her mother-in-law. Ruth's response to her
mother-in-law, after being prodded by her several times to return to her
own people, is one of the greatest expressions of loyalty that has been
recorded in the Bible:

> And Ruth said [to Naomi], Intreat me not to leave thee, or to
> return from following after thee: for whither thou goest, I will
> go; and where thou lodgest, I will lodge: thy people shall be my
> people, and thy God my God: Where thou diest, will I die, and
> there will I be buried: the Lord do so to me, and more also, if
> ought but death part thee and me. (Ruth 1:16–17 KJV)

This declaration offers the first glimpse of Ruth's selfless devotion
to Naomi, her allegiance to a "foreign" God, and her decision not
to dwell on the past, namely the loss of her husband. Amid Naomi's
the chatter, it is easy to overlook the fact that Ruth and her sister had
also suffered loss and were facing bleak futures. Orpah decided to
return to familiar surroundings and the potential protection of her
family while Ruth opted to give up everything for the unknown. Both
women made their decision without complaining about their plight of
being young widows without an inheritance or berating their almost
poverty-stricken mother-in-law. The closeness between them is obvious
because Naomi's daughters-in-law unashamedly kiss her and weep at
the thought of being separated from her. Moreover, the picture of the
three weeping together becomes more poignant as Ruth clings to her
mother-in-law, knowing Naomi had nothing to offer her in material
possessions (Ruth 1:14).

It is ironic that Ruth, of her own volition, put total trust for her future in Naomi's God while Naomi bewailed the agony that God had brought on her, failing to recognize the blessing God had given her in daughters-in-law. Naomi, in her own words, bore witness to the faithfulness of her daughters-in-law who showed kindness to her and their deceased husbands. She pointed this out on her way to Judah when she initially tried to convince her daughters-in-law to return home: "The Lord deal kindly with you, as you have dealt with the dead and with me. The Lord grant that ye may find rest, each in the house of her husband" (Ruth 1:8–9 KJV).

Bitterness blinded her eyes from seeing God's providential hand making it possible for her to return to her homeland "for she had heard in the country of Moab that the Lord had visited His people by giving them bread" (Ruth 1:6). It was the lack of bread, or famine, that initially had caused her to flee from Bethlehem, but now she returned at the time of harvest when there was an abundance of food. As would be expected, people were happy because there was prosperity and there was excitement in the air. Consequently, they warmly welcomed Naomi and her daughter-in-law. If anyone disapproved that Ruth was a Moabitess, it is not mentioned. Unfortunately, their goodwill was lost on Naomi because she had allowed ingratitude, dissatisfaction, and despair to take root in her life so her identity was distorted. She snubbed the people who greeted her—even to the point of rebuking them for addressing her by her legal name "Naomi," which means "pleasant," and insisting that they call her "Marah," which means "bitter":

> And she said unto them, Call me not Naomi, call me Mara: for the Almighty hath dealt very bitterly with me. I went out full and the Lord hath brought me home again empty: why then call ye me Naomi, seeing the Lord hath testified against me, and the Almighty hath afflicted me? (Ruth 1:20–21 KJV)

Like so many of us today who have heard the good news of salvation and felt Christ's love but continue to remain in darkness, Naomi persisted in embracing bitterness because she did not understand the scope of God's grace. During that time of Israel's history, Christ had not yet broken into history, so the concept of grace was not yet understood. The wonderful thing, however, was that God had already started the wheels that would set it in motion from the garden of Eden and would perpetuate His work indirectly through Naomi, in the person of a heathen woman called Ruth.

No reputable Jewish person would have dared to consider marrying a non-Jew, much less a Moabite. The Moabites, though connected to the Jewish people through Lot (Gen. 19:37–38), were accursed. They and the Ammonites had colluded with Balaam to curse the children of Israel before they crossed over into the Promised Land and were forbidden by God to enter the Jewish congregation up to the tenth generation (Deut. 23:3–6). Moreover, they had lured the children of Israel into idolatry and aroused God's anger against Israel (Num. 25:1–3). Lot was Abraham's nephew who accompanied him when God told Abraham to leave Ur of the Chaldees (Gen. 13:1–11). Naomi's sons most likely, if they had remained in Bethlehem, would not have not married Ruth and Orpah because they would not have received much approval from their people. However, they were in a foreign country and married women in their adopted country.

It appears that Naomi, though she had not expressed it directly, may have felt that God had afflicted her because she had allowed her sons to marry Moabite women (although good ones). The unusually good relationship and mutual affection that she shared with her daughters-in-law did not prevent her from recognizing that they would have few or no prospects of remarrying in Bethlehem, being foreigners and widows, and that she, being too old to remarry, could not reproduce eligible sons for them to marry (Ruth 1:11–13). Her appeal to her daughters-in-law to stay in their land was not only the advice of a bitter old woman who was very much aware of the gloomy prospects of surviving in a patriarchal society without a husband or sons, but it also sprang from her knowledge of God's warning to the children of Israel not to marry the people of Canaan lest they corrupt them and turn their hearts away from Him:

> When the Lord thy God shall bring thee into the land whither thou goest to possess it, and hath cast out many nations before thee, the Hittites, and the Girgashites, and the Amorites, and the Canaanites, and the Perizzites, and the Hivites, and the Jebusites, seven nations greater and mightier than thou; And when the Lord thy God shall deliver them before thee; thou shalt smite them, and utterly destroy them; thou shalt make no covenant with them, nor shew mercy unto them: Neither shalt thou make marriages with them; thy daughter thou shalt not give unto his son, nor his daughter shalt thou take unto thy son. For they will turn away thy son from following me, that they may serve other gods: so will the anger of the Lord be kindled against you, and destroy thee suddenly. But thus shall ye deal with them; ye shall destroy their altars, and break down their images, and cut down their groves, and burn their graven images with fire. (Deut. 7:1–5 KJV)

Contrary to what Naomi may have expected upon her arrival in Bethlehem, God had turned it around for her good. First, the relations between the Jews and Israelites were good considering that Naomi and her family had found refuge in Moab when she fled from the famine of the House of Bread, or Bethlehem, to Moab and the fact that both she and Ruth were cordially received upon her return. Second, God would show grace to Ruth and raise up seed through her unto Naomi so that others would declare that Ruth was better to her "than seven sons" (Ruth 4:15).

Let me glean ...

Not only did Ruth pledge her loyalty to Naomi, but she also attempted to validate her pledge by trying to eke out a living for herself and her mother-in-law. She did this by gleaning in the fields of a near kinsman of her deceased father-in-law, Elimelech, named Boaz. Fortunately, she found favor with him, and he allowed her to glean more grain than she expected. She returned home, and Naomi instructed her to woo him. Boaz was receptive to her subtle advances, but he sought to defer to a closer male relative of Elimelech to give him first place in marriage. However, the relative turned down the opportunity to marry Ruth, and Boaz happily offered his hand in marriage to her.

It is remarkable how our gifts and works go before and make room for us. Ruth had a heart of love and loyalty toward Naomi, and it motivated her to protect and provide for her. She was not daunted by the risk of going out alone to glean for grain not only in a strange city but also in a potentially dangerous field, not knowing how the owner and his workers would receive her. However, God, knowing her heart, touched the heart of Boaz who was the owner of the field and a relative of Naomi's husband. He had already heard of Ruth's loyalty and was impressed by her zeal as he told her when he met her in his field:

> And Boaz answered and said unto her, It hath fully been shewed me, all that thou hast done unto thy mother in law since the death of thine husband: and how thou hast left thy father and thy mother, and the land of thy nativity, and art come unto a people which thou knewest not heretofore. The Lord recompense thy work, and a full reward be given thee of the Lord God of Israel, under whose wings thou art come to trust. (Ruth 2:11–12 KJV)

Boaz was even more impressed that Ruth had not only left her country and voluntarily chose another people but also that she was consistent in her devotion to Naomi. Gleaning was arduous work, and it was even harder when one had to search among the pickings that the reapers had left behind. Having been made aware of her hard work in the field from morning until evening, Boaz asked his reapers to deliberately let grain fall from the bundles for her to glean and to warn his young male workers not to make unwelcome advances toward her.

> Then Boaz said to his servant who was in charge of the reapers, "Whose young woman is this?" So the servant who was in charge of the reapers answered and said, "It is the young Moabite woman who came back with Naomi from the country of Moab. And she said, 'Please let me glean and gather after the reapers among the sheaves.' So she came and has continued from morning until now, though she rested a little in the house." Then Boaz said to Ruth, "You will listen, my daughter, will you not? Do not go to glean in another field, nor go from here, but stay close by my young women. Let your eyes be on the field which they reap, and go after them. Have I not commanded the young men not to touch you? And when you are thirsty, go to the vessels and drink from what the young men have drawn." (Ruth 2:5–9 NKJV)

The picture of Ruth, resolute and steadfast in her purpose to fulfill her vow to Naomi by laboring in Boaz's field, stands in stark contrast to a scene that happened centuries before she was born. This scene involved the wife of Ruth's ancestor Lot. A flashback to the scene would have shown the smoldering plains of Sodom and Gomorrah, the screams of those trapped in the city, and the escape of Lot's family into Zoar. However, his wife did not escape the disaster. She was overcome by the burning hail and became a pillar of salt because she vacillated in her heart and disobeyed God's command not to "look back." Her disobedience led her daughters to seduce their father by making him drunk and then engaging in sexual intercourse with him. From that incestuous relationship, both daughters were impregnated and gave birth to two sons. The older daughter gave birth to Moab, father of the Moabites, and the younger gave birth to Benammi, father of the Ammonites.[2]

That one as virtuous as Ruth would have been the descendant of ancestors who committed gross impropriety is incredible. Moreover, few people would believe that a woman with her unparalleled resolve could have been related to Lot's wife, who was unable to focus on the single purpose of saving her own life. Conversely, Ruth, of her volition, vowed to give up all that she possessed, including her spiritual and material belongings, and fulfilled her vows even when she knew the outcome could have been tragic. She had the faith to believe that, in making the sacrifice to leave all that she had and committing her future to Yahweh, she would be able to change the circumstances for herself and her mother-in-law. Her faith pleased God, and He rewarded her and Naomi. On the other hand, Lot's wife did not have faith and suffered the consequence of her disbelief. Essentially, the outcomes of the two women's actions show us that faith moves God and not our needs, and that without faith it is impossible to please Him.

The kinsman-redeemer

Ruth's faith moved Boaz to action. He had heard and noticed her selflessness and sacrifice, and being a just and righteous man who was aware of the plight of Naomi and her, he felt compelled to do something about the matter. He also had familial ties to Elimelech, Naomi's husband, and therefore had some vested interest in helping his widow regain his estate, which had been sold to someone outside of the family. Since Boaz was wealthy, one of the best ways that he could preserve Elimelech's widow's inheritance was by redeeming her husband's and sons' land. Another way was to marry Ruth and raise up seed for her dead husband, Mahlon, by naming the first son from the union as the heir of the deceased.

[2.] See Genesis 19.

Marriage of his relative's widow was not obligatory, as was the situation with Tamar and Judah, since Boaz had no fraternal connections to Elimelech or his sons.

Naomi, of course, was past the age of bearing children. Ruth, having knowledge of the levirate custom, had gone to Boaz's threshing floor and, with the blessing of her mother-in-law, discreetly offered an invitation for him to take her as his wife:

> So she went down to the threshing floor and did according to all that her mother-in-law instructed her. And after Boaz had eaten and drunk, and his heart was cheerful, he went to lie down at the end of the heap of grain; and she came softly, uncovered his feet, and lay down. Now it happened at midnight that the man was startled, and turned himself; and there, a woman was lying at his feet. And he said, "Who are you?" So she answered, "I am Ruth, your maidservant. Take your maidservant under your wing, for you are a close relative." (Ruth 3:6–9 NKJV)

Although eager to help, Boaz did not attempt to go outside the conventions of his people to do so, but he deferred to another male relative to redeem Elimelech's estate and seek Ruth's hand in marriage. In the company of witnesses, Boaz asked the closer kinsman to Naomi's husband to redeem her land and the man agreed. However, on realizing that marriage to Ruth was part of the package and that his biological child would be named as the dead relative's child, he changed his mind and offered the opportunity to Boaz. Boaz, who already admired Ruth, married her and redeemed the inheritance of Elimelech and his sons.

Through the role of kinsman-redeemer that Boaz played in the lives of Ruth and Naomi, we are given a foreshadowing of the matchless work of Jesus that He would perform later in history to redeem us eternally from the kingdom of Satan into the kingdom of God. Although Boaz's action was not entirely altruistic because he was in love with Ruth, one cannot deny that he did a noble deed that would ultimately place him in the lineage of Jesus. It must be emphasized again that Boaz was not obligated under Mosaic law to marry Ruth because he was not her brother-in-law as stated in Deuteronomy 25:5–7 (NKJV):

> If brothers dwell together, and one of them dies and has no son, the widow of the dead man shall not be married to a stranger outside the family; her husband's brother shall go in to her, take her as his wife, and perform the duty of a husband's brother to her. And it shall be that the firstborn son which she bears will succeed to the name of his dead brother, that his name may not be blotted out of Israel.

Boaz chose to act on behalf of members of his family line who were unable or restricted in acting on their own behalf. In the Old Testament period of Israel, as in modern and postmodern times, situations like loss of property, poverty, death, and other unforeseen calamities occurred, and the affected parties needed others to negotiate on their behalf and even assume their responsibilities to mitigate the hardships that they faced. In the fledgling nation of Israel, there were laws to protect and preserve the property and rights of people, but the de facto execution of these laws in daily life were delimited by human weaknesses. The laws often presupposed the human factor for error in their execution and had checks in place, but they could not always anticipate the actions of a creature with free will. The law of property in Leviticus 25 counteracts coveting another's possession by outlining how one is able to redeem his own property or on behalf of another. A kinsman was usually expected to avenge the death of a relative, redeem the relative's property, or buy back his relative from slavery if he did not have the means or was unable to do so. This person was known as the *goel* or kinsman-redeemer. Boaz served as the goel for Naomi, redeeming her land since she was destitute.

The already mentioned case of Judah and Tamar shows one man's failing to honor the Hittite levirate code, which was practiced by the peoples of Canaan and predates its Deuteronomic corollary. Both levirate codes are similar but are also divergent in their purpose. Donald A. Leggett draws attention to the parallel between the two:

> The Hittite law code 42 contains one law, HC § 193, which resembles the levirate law in Israel. It reads, "If a man has a wife, and the man dies, his brother shall take his wife, then his father shall take her. If also his father dies, his brother shall take his wife (and also) the son of his brother shall (take her). (There shall be) no punishment." (1974, 21)

Judah was responsible for raising up seed for his son because he had dealt dishonestly with Tamar and reneged on his promise to give her his son to fulfill the levirate custom. Consequently, the onus rested on him to take the place of his son, which he did not relinquish to her when he came of age to marry her. The sequence of the law is that the oldest surviving brother of the defunct would marry his widow, and if he dies, the next in line would fulfill the obligation. If all surviving brothers (not brothers born after the deceased) are dead, the father must marry his son's widow or, if the father is dead, it falls to the father's brother. Therefore, Tamar was within her rights to retrieve her inheritance and perpetuate the legacy of her dead husband. Such means used by Tamar seem reprehensible to someone living in the twenty-first century, but it must be understood that a twice-childless widow in Tamar's society had no one to provide or care for her without a husband or a son who would inherit the property of her dead husband and perpetuate his name. In fact, one reason for the levirate law was to protect women and consolidate wealth in a family, from which the woman would also benefit.

Sometimes, however, the law could become unnecessary or prove burdensome for a relative. Consequently, a way of escape was created for the surviving widow to be legally released from marrying her brother-in-law and to be free to marry a man of her choice, and for the *levir* (her brother-in-law) to relinquish all rights to and responsibilities for his dead brother's property. The rite for performing the release procedure is known as *halitzah*. It is not a modified form of the levirate, and the two are not synonymous. It is better seen as a way out for a widow to garner other means for survival. Leggett points to this cause:

> The woman's initiatives make it likely that her interests were being protected by this procedure. The plight of the widow is a prominent theme in the Old Testament and we have already seen that some scholars suggest that it was the principal motive behind the levirate. If the widow waited a reasonable period without any sign that the brother-in-law was disposed to perform his duty toward her, she might, as a final measure, seek to be free from his authority and to either return to her own father or make her own way. This ceremony would then constitute a kind of release similar to the bill of divorcement. (57)

The halitzah, like marriage, was not to be entered into lightly, hence the solemnity of the manner in which it was performed in the "gate of the elders" at the request of the widow. The elders would then summon the levir, and if he refused to enter into a levirate marriage with his brother's widow, he would have to allow her to remove his shoe from his foot. Removal of the shoe by his sister-in-law was a symbolic gesture that her brother-in-law had divested himself of all rights to benefit from his brother's estate and that he had abandoned his responsibility to perpetuate his brother's name. The subsequent act of the widow spitting in her brother-in-law's face was done to shame the levir for refusing to marry her and perpetuate the name of his dead brother:

> And if the man like not to take his brother's wife, then let his brother's wife go up to the gate unto the elders, and say, My husband's brother refuseth to raise up unto his brother a name in Israel, he will not perform the duty of my husband's brother.

Then the elders of his city shall call him, and speak unto him: and if he stand to it, and say, step like not to take her; Then shall his brother's wife come unto him in the presence of the elders, and loose his shoe from off his foot, and spit in his face, and shall answer and say, So shall it be done unto that man that will not build up his brother's house. And his name shall be called in Israel, The house of him that hath his shoe loosed. (Deut. 25:7–10 NKJV)

The procedure that Boaz initiated in the city gates with the elders and near kinsman did not include all the steps of the Deuteronomic halitzah for the obvious reason: the near-kinsman was not Elimelech's, Mahlon's, or Chillon's brother and not bound by levirate law. The need to protect and provide for Naomi was more important than preserving the name of a deceased man. Therefore, more emphasis was placed on preservation of the destitute woman. Boaz, also an ancestor of Joseph, set the precedent for Joseph in seeking to protect the honor of the virtuous Virgin Mary. When Ruth came to Boaz's threshing floor, he was careful to make sure that she would not be disgraced. He assured her, "Let it not be known that a woman came into the floor" (Ruth 3:14, NKJV). Joseph, after finding out that Mary was pregnant and knowing that he was not the father of her child, did not attempt to disgrace or punish her but decided to put her away secretly. Fortunately, God revealed to him in a dream that the Holy Ghost had wrought the conception of the babe in her womb. Boaz also made sure that Ruth would not be disgraced after she slipped into his threshing floor at night while he was sleeping and proposed marriage to him. Boaz could not have loved her more than at that moment, feeling a sense of joy that she would pursue him and not any of the younger men in that city. Therefore, he said to her:

"The Lord bless you, my daughter," he replied. "This kindness is greater than that which you showed earlier: You have not run after the younger men, whether rich or poor. And now, my daughter, don't be afraid. I will do for you all you ask. All the people of my town know that you are a woman of noble character (Ruth 3:10–11 NKJV)

He watched her, dressed in her best clothes, and smelled the waft of her perfume, but he would not tarnish her good name by sleeping with her before following the appropriate conventions. Instead he made sure she had enough food to eat and that whatever decisions he would make concerning her would be in her best interest:

> Although it is true that I am a guardian-redeemer of our family, there is another who is more closely related than I. Stay here for the night, and in the morning if he wants to do his duty as your guardian-redeemer, good; let him redeem you. But if he is not willing, as surely as the Lord lives I will do it. Lie here until morning. So she lay at his feet until morning, but got up before anyone could be recognized; and he said, "No one must know that a woman came to the threshing floor." He also said, "Bring me the shawl you are wearing and hold it out." When she did so, he poured into it six measures of barley and placed the bundle on her. Then he went back to town. (Ruth 3:12–15 NKJV)

Boaz, though startled by Ruth's presence in his threshing floor, did not seem unnerved by her sexual overtures toward him. On the contrary, he insisted on reminding her of her virtue and nobility of character. Her "act of seduction" was not considered inappropriate since, as a widow with pure motives to preserve Elimelech's and her husband's lineage, she had approached her deceased husband's relative with Naomi's consent to try to convince him to fulfill the levirate custom. Ruth was careful not to reveal who she was until Boaz had finished eating and drinking, hoping that with a full stomach and being happy with wine, he would be more inclined to consider her request (Ruth 3:7). Obviously, she had been watching him before he went to lie down and picked the right time to enter the threshing floor because her mother-in-law had prepared her for the occasion:

> Then it shall be, when he lies down, that you shall notice the place where he lies; and you shall go in, uncover his feet, and lie down; and he will tell you what you should do. (Ruth 3:4 NKJV)

When Ruth approached Boaz, she did not know the outcome of her action. She had had short conversations with him and he had shown concern for her and Naomi's needs, but she was taking a big risk by entering his threshing floor without being invited. Boaz, who was about twice her age and still virile, was reputed to be an honorable man ... But who could be sure what a man, somewhat disoriented from sleep and perhaps a little inebriated from drinking, would do to an attractive woman lying at his feet at night?

Naomi was surely a good judge of Boaz's character and must have regained her faith in God because she would not have encouraged her beloved daughter-in-law to risk her reputation for the redemption of her land. What would ensue in the scene of the threshing floor would be totally different from what took place in the cave of Zoar with Ruth's predecessors (Gen. 19:32–33). Boaz, unlike Lot, was not drunk and was fully in control of his faculties. Neither was Ruth's motive to make him drunk like Lot's daughters had or to seduce him as Tamar did to Judah, but to bring a matter to him at the most appropriate time and place to increase the potential for the desired outcome. As a matter of fact, because she wanted him to make a commitment to her, she made her intentions very clear to him. She did what was necessary to send the message to Boaz that she was romantically interested in him without dishonoring herself.

It took the resolve of a godly man to uphold his honor and the honor of a woman to whom he was attracted and not to satisfy his carnal desires if given the opportunity. He suppressed his own desires and, being fully aware of the implications for the parties involved if the matter was not addressed, decided to settle the matter in a legal manner. Like Ruth, Boaz placed the need of someone else above himself. He lived during the time of the judges, when Israel was in a stasis of moral decay and everyone did what was right in his own eyes. Yet even against that backdrop of rebellion, idolatry, and uncertainty, Boaz represented what Psalm 1 so clearly states:

> Blessed is the man
> Who walks not in the counsel of the ungodly,
>
> Nor stands in the path of sinners,
> Nor sits in the seat of the scornful;
>
> But his delight is in the law of the Lord,
>
> And in His law he meditates day and night.
>
> (v.1–2 NKJV)

Unfortunately, his great-grandson King David did not follow the precedent of his predecessor and committed adultery with the wife of one of his soldiers, incurring the judgment of God on himself, his family, and his people (II Samuel 2). His lapse in judgment cost him his peace and tore his family apart, although God remembered his righteousness and was still gracious to him. He had not learned from the lesson of Boaz and Ruth that making godly decisions, even when faced with the urge for immediate gratification, would surely bring joy and peace in the end. David paid the price for his folly during most of his reign; Boaz, on the other hand, enjoyed an idyllic life with Ruth in his old age.

Here is my shoe ...

God commanded Moses to take off his shoes when Moses noticed a bush that was aflame but did not burn, and he drew closer to see this magnificent sight. Moses obeyed the voice of God, removed his shoes, and even hid his face for he was afraid in the presence of the Almighty (Exod. 3:6). It was the consummate act of humility.

A similar act took place in the city gates of Bethlehem-Judah, though for different reasons: The closer kinsman of Naomi removed his shoe to free himself from the responsibility of the levirate law in response to Boaz's request that he marry Ruth. The kinsman, though agreeing to redeem the land for Naomi, was reluctant to jeopardize his own inheritance by fathering a potential offspring of Ruth's dead husband if he should marry her. Boaz showed himself not only to be a pious man but also to be very shrewd by the manner in which he negotiated the rights of inheritance with his near kinsman. Nevertheless, we cannot forget that he had divine guidance. He avoided mentioning Ruth when he initiated the subject of near kinsman responsibility and spoke only about redeeming the land of Elimelech for impoverished Naomi:

> Now Boaz went up to the gate and sat down there; and behold, the close relative of whom Boaz had spoken came by. So Boaz said, "Come aside, friend, sit down here." So he came aside and sat down. And he took ten men of the elders of the city, and said, "Sit down here." So they sat down. Then he said to the close relative, "Naomi, who has come back from the country of Moab, sold the piece of land which belonged to our brother Elimelech. And I thought to inform you, saying, 'Buy it back in the presence of the inhabitants and the elders of my people. If you will redeem it, redeem it; but if you will not redeem it, then tell me, that I may know; for there is no one but you to redeem it, and I am next after you.'" And he said, "I will redeem it." (Ruth 4:1–4, NKJV)

Knowing human nature, Boaz had perhaps anticipated that the near kinsman would have shown empathy for Naomi and agreed to redeem her land. However, since the matter of Ruth could be a tricky one (because, in fact, the kinsman was not bound to marry her, according to Jewish law), he broached the subject only after receiving an affirmative from his near-kinsman about redemption of the land:

> Then Boaz said, "On the day you buy the field from the hand of Naomi, you must also buy it from Ruth the Moabitess, the wife of the dead, to perpetuate the name of the dead through his inheritance." And the close relative said, "I cannot redeem it for myself, lest I ruin my own inheritance. You redeem my right of redemption for yourself, for I cannot redeem it." (Ruth 4:5–6 NKJV)

By delaying the request for Ruth's marriage, Boaz endeavored to accomplish two things: to be able to help his near-kinsman save face if he declined his offer and to prove to Ruth that he was willing to marry her, not only to fulfill his obligation as a kinsman-redeemer but also because he truly valued her as a person.

According to the levirate, the widow would have to initiate the request for the elders to summon the near-kinsman to marry her. She would also remove the shoe and spit in his face if rejected and say, "So shall it be done unto that man that will not build up his brother's house" (Deut. 25:9), since it was the widow who was forbidden to marry until the halitzah was performed. Although the levir would be disgraced, the ritual was inherently shameful for both parties since it would be hard to find many women who would relish having to pull off a man's shoe in public and emit spit—not to mention having to air such delicate conversation in front of the elders and people of the city!

Neither Ruth nor the near-kinsman was humiliated. The near-kinsman was not unshod by Ruth; rather he voluntarily removed his shoe and offered it to a joyful Boaz. Boaz resolved the situation amicably and with the goodwill of his near kinsman:

> Now this was the custom in former times in Israel concerning redeeming and exchanging, to confirm anything: one man took off his sandal and gave it to the other, and this was a confirmation in Israel. (Ruth 4:7 NKJV)

> Therefore, the close relative said to Boaz, "Buy it for yourself." So he took off his sandal. And Boaz said to the elders and all the people, "You are witnesses this day that I have bought all that was Elimelech's, and all that was Chilion's and Mahlon's, from the hand of Naomi. Moreover, Ruth the Moabitess, the widow of Mahlon, I have acquired as my wife, to perpetuate the name of the dead through his inheritance, that the name of the dead may not be cut off from among his brethren and from his position at the gate. You are witnesses this day." (Ruth 4:8–10 NKJV)

Boaz thus saved Ruth from the ignominy of being a spectacle, preserved her honor, secured the estate of Elimelech, and restored the fortune of Naomi. For himself, he gained a virtuous woman whose "price was far above rubies" (Prov. 31:10). Yet God had even greater blessings by giving them a son named Obed, not only to raise up seed for the dead but also to continue the royal line of David.

> And all the people who were at the gate, and the elders, said, "We are witnesses. The Lord make the woman who is coming to your house like Rachel and Leah, the two who built the house of Israel; and may you prosper in Ephrathah and be famous in Bethlehem. May your house be like the house of Perez, whom Tamar bore to Judah, because of the offspring which the Lord will give you from this young woman." (Ruth 4:11–12 NKJV)

It was Boaz and not Mahlon, and Judah, not Er, who would be recorded in the genealogy of David and ultimately Jesus Christ (Matt. 1). Both men, not knowing that in doing daily activities, both bad and good, would have been used to carry out God's plan. It is not that God engineered the actions that Tamar and Judah engaged in, but He, by His sovereign hand, intervened and fulfilled his purpose. In the same vein, the names of three known foreign women—Tamar, Rahab, and Ruth— became mothers of the ancestors of our Lord and Savior. Bathsheba, one of King David's wives, is the only other woman mentioned with them in Matthew:

> Judah begot Perez and Zerah by Tamar, Perez begot Hezron, and Hezron begot Ram. Ram begot Amminadab, Amminadab begot Nahshon, and Nahshon begot Salmon. Salmon begot Boaz by Rahab, Boaz begot Obed by Ruth, Obed begot Jesse, and Jesse begot David the king. David the king begot Solomon by her who had been the wife of Uriah. (Matt. 1:3–6 NKJV)

It must not be taken lightly that these women of dubious backgrounds are listed in Matthew's Gospel. Even the secular world would question their backgrounds, yet they are included in the annals of the history of Christ's genealogy. God shows us that even before He sent Jesus to die for us on the cross and impart grace in its fullness, He was already showing it to whomever was willing to seek Him. Paul, in Romans 2:10–11, confers "glory, honor, and peace, to every man that worketh good, to the Jew first, and also to the Gentile" because he notes, "There is no respect of persons with God." Ruth was from an idolatrous nation, but she made a conscious decision to choose the eternal God. The Almighty Jehovah counted it for righteousness as He did with Abraham and honored her for it.

CHAPTER 8

Bathsheba

Bathsheba is one of the most vilified and fascinating women of the Bible. However, little is known about her life apart from David, except that she was married to Uriah, the Hittite who was among the thirty-seven "mighty men"[3] in David's army. She had no children before she married David but bore him four sons: Shobab, Shimea, Nathan, and Solomon.[4] Her father's name was Ammiel,[5] the son of Ahithophel, the trusted advisor to King David who later betrayed him.[6] Since her grandfather was an important member of the king's cabinet and her father was one of "the thirty-seven elite fighting men" (2 Sam. 23:14) in David's army, we may infer that she was from an influential family.

It should come as no surprise then that Bathsheba, being connected to Ahithophel, would have learned the art of diplomacy, a skill that served her well in grooming and securing Solomon's ascendancy to the throne of David. Additionally, it enhanced her position as queen mother during his reign as ruler over the United Kingdom of Israel and Judah.

Having been blessed with remarkable allure, she joins the ranks of other Old Testament women like Sarah and Rachel who were

---

3. 1 Chronicles 11:41 and 2 Samuel 23:38
4. See 1 Chronicles 3:5.
5. See 1 Chronicles 3:5 and 2 Samuel 23:34. Note that Ammiel is also called Eliam.
6. See 2 Samuel 15:12, 31–37; and 2 Samuel 17: 1–23. Also see Psalm 41:9 and 55:12–14.

known for their exceptional beauty. Though she lacks the notoriety of the villainous Jezebel,[7] she is sometimes portrayed as the seductress who tempted David and tarnished his kingdom. She was a victim of circumstances who found herself in the right place at the wrong time— she performed her purification rite at a time when the king had too much time on his hands!

> Then it happened one evening that David arose from his bed and walked on the roof of the king's house. And from the roof he saw a woman bathing, and the woman was very beautiful to behold. So David sent and inquired about the woman. And someone said, "Is this not Bathsheba, the daughter of Eliam, the wife of Uriah the Hittite?" Then David sent messengers, and took her; and she came to him, and he lay with her, for she was cleansed from her impurity; and she returned to her house. And the woman conceived; so she sent and told David, and said, "I am with child." (2 Sam. 11:2–5 NKJV)

Her story is in some way a haunting reminder of Jephthah's daughter in the book of Judges who was in the right place at the wrong time. Her father had been successful in a war against the Ammonites and had rashly made a vow that whatever came out of the door first to meet him after his victory would be sacrificed to God. Unfortunately, his teenage daughter was the first one who came out to greet him with dancing and singing. Jephthah regretted his decision; however, he did not rescind his vow nor appeal to God; rather he sacrificed his daughter to fulfill his oath.

It was expected of women in Bathsheba's day to take a bath for hygienic purposes as well as to satisfy the rite of purification after completing their menstrual cycle. Apparently, Bathsheba was taking one of those baths without being aware that the king was watching her. First, from

---

[7.] 1 Kings 21:1–16 and 2 Kings 9:33

what she knew about fighting men, since her father and her husband were high-ranking officers, it was unusual for kings to be hanging around their palaces during a time of war. As a matter of fact, because David was commander-in-chief of the Israelite army, it was especially out of character for him, a seasoned man of war, to remain idle while his army was battling the Ammonites:

> It happened in the spring of the year, at the time when kings go out to battle, that David sent Joab and his servants with him, and all Israel; and they destroyed the people of Ammon and besieged Rabbah. But David remained at Jerusalem. (2 Sam. 11:1 NKJV)

Second, Bathsheba would have done her ceremonial washing every month in the privacy of her home or with other women in a communal bath known as a *mitzvah*. A menstruating woman and one who had completed her cycle for less than seven days were considered to have defiled any surface or person with which or whom she came in contact. Few men, if any, would want to be caught in the uncompromising position of being near an unclean woman or even peeping at her because she was considered ceremonially unclean. Therefore, Bathsheba would not have expected voyeurism from anyone, especially not the much loved and respected king. Most likely, it would not have crossed her mind that the king would have summoned her to his palace for frivolous reasons and not for a serious issue, considering that her husband and father served in the Israelite army.

There is some speculation about the role that Bathsheba played in initiating her illicit affair with David, and also her knowledge or lack of knowledge in the subterfuge that led to the death of her husband. Although she was not an ingenue, Bathsheba was surely not in a position of power in the presence of a persistent, "lust-driven" king; therefore, it must have been hard to resist his sexual advances. She must have been shocked when she found out his motive for summoning her to the palace, considering he was aware of her marital status and her family connections. Few women, if any, in her situation could have easily escaped the cunning of a formidable military man who had consistently outwitted his enemies and won so many victories on the battlefield.

We cannot be sure why she did not vehemently protest or call for help, but there are some reasons that come to mind. One of the most obvious is that, as a commoner (though of a privileged background) and a woman, she was afraid to assert herself in the presence of the king. She also may have thought that David could bring reprisals against her husband if she did not cooperate with him. And as shocking as it may sound, she may have seen it as a privilege to be desired by the ruler of Judah and Israel! He may have stirred a passion in her ignited by her longing for her husband, who was most likely separated from her for long periods because of his commitment to his military duties. Uriah's response to David after the king offered him leave and pressured him to go home to spend time with Bathsheba testifies to his dedication to his vocation, even placing it above family and his own personal pleasure:

> And David said to Uriah, "Go down to your house and wash your feet." So Uriah departed from the king's house, and a gift of food from the king followed him. But Uriah slept at the door of the king's house with all the servants of his lord, and did not go down to his house. So when they told David, saying, "Uriah did not go down to his house," David said to Uriah, "Did you not come from a journey? Why did you not go down to your house?" And Uriah said to David, "The ark and Israel and Judah are dwelling in tents, and my lord Joab and the servants of my lord are encamped in the open fields. Shall I then go to my house to eat and drink, and to lie with my wife? As you live, and as your soul lives, I will not do this thing." (2 Sam. 11:8–11 NKJV)

Uriah's response to David's adamant requests stands in contrast to his wife's resignation toward the king's sexual advances. Both Uriah and

Bathsheba were subordinates of the king and therefore subject to his authority. However, Uriah, a Hittite who by choice had converted to Judaism, chose to honor the law when the king's word was not aligned with the word of God. Bathsheba, on the hand, may have allowed fear to prevent her from opposing the king in his intent to commit sin. Uriah showed the utmost respect to David, but he insisted on doing what was right. He appealed to the virtues of honesty, loyalty, and honor that he had seen in David before he became king. These qualities and the zeal to protect the name of God may have been the factors that motivated Uriah and other "heads of the mighty men whom David had, who strengthened themselves with him in his kingdom, with all Israel, to make him king, according to the word of the Lord concerning Israel" to follow him (1 Chron. 11:10). Uriah's mention of "the ark dwelling in tents" was an allusion to God—a hint that was lost on the otherwise righteous David, who was now driven by his motivation to cover his sin. In essence Uriah had disobeyed the ultimate head of his army and his kingdom because of his godly character. Under normal circumstances, David could have punished him for insubordination, but had he done that, his guilt would have been exposed. How would he justify sentencing a man to death for showing him loyalty?

Despite David's heinous act, Bathsheba's situation did not absolve her of wrongdoing, although the greater sin lay with him. Unfortunately, she is sometimes viewed as more culpable than David despite the fact that he initiated the actions that led to adultery and the death of a righteous man. No one understood the role of a shepherd like David because he was the shepherd boy who was tending the sheep when the prophet Samuel anointed him to succeed Saul as king. He was the one who penned the twenty-third psalm and described the Lord as our ultimate shepherd who completely protects His sheep. Therefore, it came as no surprise that Nathan would use "the ewe lamb" as a metaphor for Bathsheba to show her vulnerability as he wove the story to David of a rich man who takes the only lamb that his neighbor owns and prepares it for the wayfarer, despite the fact that the rich man has more than enough ewe lambs of his own (2 Sam. 12). Ironically, it was the man whom God had placed as the shepherd of His people of Israel who became the "wolf that attacks the sheep," so there was no protection.

Come, lie with me

David pursued Bathsheba with almost the same zeal he would have had if pursuing an enemy, except his motive toward her was different. The same doggedness that propelled him to kill Goliath and overcome the lion and the bear that attacked his flock when he was a shepherd was also unleashed in his hunger for Bathsheba. On the battlefield, that was an admirable character trait, but the same trait led to his downfall when he used it to take another man's property and shed innocent blood. Even after finding out that the object of his desire was the wife of one of the valiant officers who had given him "strong support in his kingdom, together with Israel, to make him king according to the word of the Lord concerning Israel" (1 Chron. 11:10, NASB), he was not deterred from his purpose.

It is obvious from David's reaction that he had not given great thought to the consequences of his action and their effect on his family and the children of Israel. Having had firsthand knowledge of the ways of God, he failed to recognize that God would punish sin. He allowed his desires to consume him so much, he did not consider that Bathsheba was of childbearing age, that she probably was in her most fertile phase, and that she could become pregnant if he had sexual intercourse with her. The fact that he spied her doing her cleansing ritual was evidence that her period was over and it was a time when her husband would be able to lie with her had he not been defending Israel!

It was after David received word from her of her pregnancy that he started devising ways to cover his adultery because he began to see the implications of his action. He had sent her home after lying with her, perhaps intending to recall her to the palace whenever he desired without being found out. However, her pregnancy and the integrity of the godly Uriah foiled his plans. Sadly, righteous David, who had had several opportunities in the past to kill Saul even in self-defense and restrained himself on every occasion, was the same man who plotted the murder of a loyal subject in order to have his wife.

The question we should ask ourselves is "How could God's chosen king commit such an atrocity in Israel after experiencing his power?" He had seen the wrath of God on Saul and his house for his disobedience and had also experienced the blessings on those who were obedient. However, he tested God by doing specific things named in the Ten Commandments (Exod. 20:1–10) that the children of Israel were told not to do. The first sin was covetousness and then subsequent acts of adultery and murder. In the book of James, the writer tells us that lust can lead to great sin and even death when we allow it to flourish in our hearts. King David allowed his eyes to lure him into activities that he detested. However, by giving in to lust, he was drawn away by his own passions and experienced what James warns us about:

> But each one is tempted when he is drawn away by his own desires and enticed. Then, when desire has conceived, it gives birth to sin; and sin, when it is full-grown brings forth death. (James 1:14–15 NKJV)

David's sin is a reminder to us that the ostensibly harmless things we do are the starting point for greater sin. We must be proactive in avoiding situations that, although not harmful, may be potential catalysts for dangerous activities. For example, David did not commit sin by not joining his army in the battle against the Ammonites, but it was the expectation that he would have been with them. The Bible does not record that he was sick or even exhausted and therefore had to recuperate at home. It appears that he was "suffering from a case of ennui" by having had too much time on his hands and sought diversion by walking about on his roof.

His eyes surveyed the view below and fell upon the form of a beautiful woman. Apparently, he did not have the will to pull them away from the unsuspecting stranger engaged in her private activity. He then began to desire her so he sought her personal data. Having found out that she was another's wife was not a roadblock for David because desire had already given way to sin. He was already on a slippery slope to satisfy his obsession and experience the inevitable: spiritual separation from God.

In that place of separation David was unable to hear the voice of God as he continued to sink deeper into the mire of sin. God, knowing the human heart better than David knew it, confronted David with his sin by sending the prophet Nathan to speak to him. Nathan drew David's attention to his sin by using a parable that compared him to a rich man who stole a poor man's only sheep and slaughtered it to prepare food for a traveler. David quickly condemned the rich man's action and suggested that he immediately be put to death. When Nathan told him he was the rich man who had stolen Uriah's wife and had him killed with the sword of the Ammonites, the king admitted his transgression and repented.

David's own heart had to condemn him so he could see that "the wrath of God is revealed from heaven against all ungodliness and unrighteousness of men, who hold the truth in unrighteousness" (Rom. 1:18 KJV). He saw clearly that he had sinned against God, and that through his wicked deed, he had shown to the enemies of God that he despised the anointing that God had placed on him as leader of Israel and Judah. As Paul said so eloquently in Romans, David's heart must have cried out when confronted with the weight of his sin: "Therefore you are inexcusable, O man, whoever you are who judge: for in whatever you judge another, you condemn yourself; for you who judge practice the same things" (Rom. 2:2 NKJV). Hence, he was forced to utter these words in contrition: "Against thee, thee only, have I sinned, and done this evil in thy sight" (Ps. 51:4 KJV).

God forgave him, but God is a God of judgment: He expects His commands to be followed because they are immutable. After God descended on Mount Sinai to verbalize His commandments to the children of Israel,[8] He also penned his words on tablets of stone and gave them to Moses in order to ensure that the Israelites would understand those words clearly and not sin against Him (Exod. 31:18). Therefore, God spelled out His directives clearly and succinctly:

> Thou shalt not kill. Thou shalt not commit adultery. Thou shalt not steal. Thou shalt not bear false witness against thy neighbor. Thou shalt not covet thy neighbour's house, thou shalt not covet thy neighbour's wife, nor his manservant, nor his maidservant, nor his ox, nor his ass, nor any thing that is thy neighbour's. (Exod. 20:13–14 KJV)

If there was one who was familiar with the law of God, it was David. Therefore, there was no excuse for his well-calculated action, and God was displeased. He would show David and all peoples that He was no respecter of persons and sin would be punished, especially to those who had been given the authority to rule over His people. Moses was God's chosen leader of the Israelites, yet God did not withhold his punishment when Moses disobeyed Him at the waters of Meribah despite the fact that Moses was provoked to anger by the children of Israel. Their constant complaining caused him to fail to perform God's instruction and as a consequence of this spiritual *faux pas* was prohibited from entering the Promised Land (Num. 20:2–13). If God did not spare meek Moses, therefore He would punish David for coveting and stealing another man's wife, committing adultery with her, and spilling innocent blood to hide his sin. Furthermore, David caused the enemies of God to speak disparagingly against God's Holy Name. The punishment would fit the crime: God meted out to him

---

[8.] See Exodus 19–20. God did not permit Moses to be His mouthpiece here. He came down to Mount Sinai and spoke to the children of Israel from a smoky cloud. After His speech, he gave Moses tablets of stone on which the commandments were written.

publicly what he had done to Uriah in secret. The prophet Nathan proclaimed God's sentence on His chosen king—the man whom God chose over Saul:

> "Why have you despised the commandment of the Lord, to do evil in His sight? You have killed Uriah the Hittite with the sword; you have taken his wife to be your wife, and have killed him with the sword of the people of Ammon. Now therefore, the sword shall never depart from your house, because you have despised Me, and have taken the wife of Uriah the Hittite to be your wife." Thus says the Lord: "Behold, I will raise up adversity against you from your own house; and I will take your wives before your eyes and give them to your neighbor, and he shall lie with your wives in the sight of this sun. For you did it secretly, but I will do this thing before all Israel, before the sun." So David said to Nathan, "I have sinned against the Lord." And Nathan said to David, "The Lord also has put away your sin; you shall not die. However, because by this deed you have given great occasion to the enemies of the Lord to blaspheme, the child also who is born to you shall surely die." Then Nathan departed to his house. (2 Sam. 12:9–15 NKJV)

Moreover, what shame and embarrassment Bathsheba must have also felt after others (father and grandfather) found out that she had slept with King David. At the time that the prophet Nathan revealed David's sin to him, Bathsheba was already David's wife and living at the palace; therefore, she would have realized the shocking truth that the king had had a hand in the death of her husband, Uriah, and that he had not died as a casualty of war. How was she able to bear the stares, whispers, and scorn of the king's other wives, the palace staff, and the general populace? It must have been hard to face her relatives knowing that she may have been the object of both their pity and ire because of the magnitude of her transgression.

The scandalous act between her and David was not only known in the kingdom of Israel and Judah but was also spread beyond their borders. It had become the conversation piece of the enemies of Israel as they gloated over David's sin. The notorious warrior-king would have been admired, hated, and feared by surrounding nations because of the many victories God had given him. One Chronicles 14:17 bears out this presumption: "And the fame of David went out into all the lands; and the Lord brought fear of him upon all nations." The prophet Nathan told David that his act gave the enemies of God a reason to disrespect his name; therefore, the child born from his adulterous relationship with Bathsheba would die:

> And Nathan said to David, "The Lord also has put away your sin; you shall not die. However, because by this deed you have given great occasion to the enemies of the Lord to blaspheme, the child also who is born to you shall surely die. (2 Sam. 13–15 NKJV)

Although God had forgiven David and Bathsheba of their sin, He would not allow them to enjoy the "fruit of their adulterous union." In the same way He told Joshua that the "accursed thing" had to be put away from the community of Israel after they went up against Ai the first time, so the child had to die in order for full reconciliation to occur in the lives of David and Bathsheba. Now, imagine Bathsheba trying to cope with all the consequences of her relationship with King David and experiencing pregnancy at the same time. Her journey could not have been smooth although she was able to have her baby. However, the presence of this child would have been a glaring reminder of her salacious past and her "sin would ever be before [her]"(Ps. 51:2); therefore, God took the child. He restored blessings to her and David and later gave them four sons, one of whom became the successor to the throne of David. Another son, Nathan, is believed to be Mary's ancestor and is mentioned in Luke's genealogical account of Christ.

Bathsheba's life with David started out on a rocky path and continued to be bittersweet for the rest of her life with him. They would experience situations as a natural consequence of and for the fulfillment of God's judgment on David for the transgression they had committed toward Uriah, the Hittite. Bathsheba would suffer guilt, at least during the first part of her marriage to David—guilt regarding her adultery, the murder of her husband, and the illegitimate conception and death of her first child. Being a part of the royal household and a wife of David, she was not unscathed by the scandalous acts and the open rebellion of his sons. It was hard enough seeing the fulfillment of Nathan's prophecy, but nothing prepared her for the attempt on David's life and the subterfuge carried out against him by those closest to him, including her own grandfather, Ahithophel.

Ahithophel was such a trusted and respected advisor that "[his] counsel, which he counseled in those days, was as if a man had enquired of the oracle of God: so was all the counsel of Ahithophel with David and Absalom" (2 Sam.16:23). Bathsheba, like most of Israel, would have looked up to Ahithophel for his wise counsel, and most likely was proud of his wisdom. We do not know if she was aware, as some believe, that he may have harbored a grudge against David for the shame he had brought on her and for the king's complicity in the death of her husband. However, Ahithophel conspired with Absalom to disgrace and kill David. When his plans were foiled by Hushai, the Archite, a loyal friend of David, Ahithophel killed himself. No words can truly express Bathsheba's feelings of shame, grief, anger, and frustration, and even a sense of relief for the life of her king and lover being saved from the destruction that was planned against him.

Despite the turmoil and pain in her life, Bathsheba was able to find refuge in the "shadow of the Almighty" (Ps. 91:1). Living so closely to the king, she learned that "as the hart panteth after the water brooks, so panteth his soul after God" (Ps. 42:1). She learned that David was truly "a man after God's own heart." From his example, she learned about the grace and forgiveness of God and that those He loves, He chastens. The God who brought judgment on the house of David was the same God who blessed her with four sons, including Solomon (Jedediah), who became the wealthiest and wisest man on earth. Bathsheba also developed a strong friendship with Nathan, which served her well in securing Solomon's ascension to the throne of David. She emerged as David's favorite wife and the most influential in his life—even more than Abigail, who showed kindness to David when he was running away from Saul and camped near Carmel. Her husband, Nabal, refused to give David help when he requested it.

David married several wives before Bathsheba, including Abigail, Ahinoam, Maacah, Haggith, Eglah, and Michal, daughter of King Saul. Haggith's son, Adonijah, was David's oldest living son and heir apparent to the throne; however, David did not choose him to be his successor. Instead he chose Bathsheba's son to sit on his throne in order to honor the oath he had sworn to her. We learn later that it was God's will for Solomon to succeed his father regardless of his mother's efforts. Adonijah testified that it was through divine intervention that Solomon became king when he came to seek Bathsheba's help to ask her son to give him Abishag, David's concubine, to be his wife:

> And he said, Thou knowest that the kingdom was mine, and that all Israel set their faces on me, that I should reign: howbeit the kingdom is turned about, and is become my brother's: for it was his from the Lord. (1 Kings 2:15 KJV)

That Adonijah would seek Bathsheba to speak for him before King Solomon to request the concubine of their deceased father shows he recognized that she could strongly influence her son. Because he knew Solomon's affection for his mother, he hoped that by having her approach the king on his behalf, he would not elicit Solomon's ire for making such a request. Solomon was not to be placated, and Adonijah was killed for his audacity. However, the king's reception of his mother expressly revealed his deep affection for her and affirmed her position as "Queen Mother":

> Bathsheba therefore went unto King Solomon, to speak unto him for Adonijah. And the king rose up to meet her, and bowed himself unto her, and sat down on his throne, and caused a seat to be set for the king's mother; and she sat on his right hand. (1 Kings 2:19 NKJV)

For most of her adult life with David, Bathsheba would experience the joy of being the king's favorite wife and at the same time bear the repercussions of past actions. She was shielded from some of the treachery that occurred during her husband's reign because many of David's enemies were already dead or had been killed by Solomon at the beginning of his reign. Therefore, she was able to reap the benefits of being the mother of the wisest and wealthiest king in the known world. Moreover, her son was king when Israel and Judah were no longer threatened by enemy nations: David had brought rest to his kingdom by defeating those nations. He subdued many of the neighboring countries that terrorized Israel, including the formidable Philistines, and made it possible for Solomon to enjoy peace throughout his reign just as the Lord had promised:

> Behold, a son shall be born to you, who shall be a man of rest; and I will give him rest from all his enemies all around. His name shall be Solomon, for I will give peace and quietness to Israel in his days. He shall build a house for My name, and he shall be My son, and I will be his Father; and I will establish the throne of his kingdom over Israel forever. (1 Chron. 22:9 –10 NKJV):

Bathsheba may not have been able to change her past and its effect, but she was able to learn from her error. Had she not learned from the error of her past, she would not have had the honor of being mentioned in the genealogical account of Matthew. She is the only Jewish[9] woman among the four listed in Matthew's account: Tamar was a Canaanite, Rahab was from Jericho, and Ruth was a Moabite. However, it is interesting to note that all four women were named in Matthew's genealogical account except Bathsheba. She was not named but was alluded to as "her who had been the wife of Uriah" to be the mother of Solomon, begat by King David (Matt. 1:3). Luke's Gospel only includes the patrilineal lineage of Jesus and not the matrilineal, in keeping with Jewish custom. Therefore, it is significant that Matthew included the names of women in his familial tabulation—and to say the least, women with questionable backgrounds.

The fact that Matthew listed the names of women, and socially undesirable women, in his account tells us that the omission of Bathsheba's name and inclusion of Uriah's name was not an error on the part of Matthew. No specific answer is given, but we are aware that with Uriah's untimely death brought on by the machination of David, he did not have the opportunity to procreate and perpetuate his name. It may therefore be an attempt on the part of the writer to remind us of his life by mentioning him by name in the royal line of King David. God told Cain in Genesis 4:10 that the voice of the blood of Abel cried out to him from the grave after Cain murdered his brother. In the same way, the voice of the blood of Uriah cried out to be avenged, and God became displeased with David. Not only would God punish David but He also would inspire Matthew to include the name of Uriah with his and Solomon's name in the Davidic family tree so his righteousness would not be forgotten.

Like Rahab, who carries the appendage of harlot even today, Bathsheba will sometimes be remembered as the seductress who brought about the beginning of the upheaval in David's kingdom, and not only as

---

[9]. It is assumed that Bathsheba was a Jew, but the Bible does not state that directly. Her grandfather Ahitophel was from Giloh, a part of Judah, so she may be from David's tribe.

David's wife but also as the wife of Uriah, the Hittite. Depending on the perspective of the reader, she may be viewed negatively as a manipulative temptress who lured David into sin, which ultimately destroyed his monarchy, or she may be seen as the vulnerable young woman who fell into sin, repented, and was blessed by God to join the ranks of other women of old who would be receivers of His grace to fulfill His purpose on earth.

CHAPTER 9

Rahab, the Harlot

> By faith the harlot Rahab did not perish with those who did not
> believe, when she had received the spies with peace. (Heb. 11:31)

Rahab has pride of place among women of the Bible. She is one of the
four women mentioned in the genealogical tree of Jesus Christ and one
among the three whose names are listed. As was noted in a previous
chapter, the names of Rahab, Tamar, and Ruth are listed among Jesus's
male predecessors in the book of Matthew; Bathsheba is mentioned as
the wife of Uriah, but her name is not given. Rahab is also mentioned
in the Hall of Faith in Hebrews 11:31 among Old Testament stalwarts
of faith like Abraham, Isaac, Jacob, Joseph, and Moses. Except for Sarah
(Heb. 11:11), Rahab is the only woman included in the lineup of the
faithful because when "that which may be known of God [was] manifest
in [her]; for God hath shewed it unto [her]" (Rom. 1:19 KJV), she
believed and acted on it.

She was a citizen of Jericho, one of the oldest civilizations on earth.
Elizabeth Fletcher (2006) posits that "[this city] was already five
thousand years old when Joshua arrived" and that its history can be
traced back to 9,000 BC. She further states that the city had a history
of various attacks "by conquerors who tramped in with their armies
and razed the town to the ground because it had a favorable location."
She also notes, "Jericho was a magnet." For that reason, it is safe to

believe that Rahab may have been able to set up a brothel on the outer area within the city walls to garner business from travelers who were drawn to the city. What circumstances led her into a life of harlotry and away from the family she loved so dearly are unknown to us. However, considering that women had few or no choices to make a living then, she may have fallen into prostitution by necessity.

We may also conclude that Rahab supplemented her "less than honorable trade" by dabbling in cloth making because she had swathes of flax laid out on her roof for drying. They came in handy for covering the spies when the king of Jericho's messengers came to seek them. Rahab meticulously placed the flax in the manner that someone who was familiar with retting would have done. Retting was a method of laying pieces of flax on a surface for several days to allow it to be humidified by dew. The dew would cause the stem of the flax to separate from the stalk. The separated stalk held fibers that would be further separated, dried, beaten, and spun into linen. That the king's messengers did not find it odd that she had neatly spread flax on her roof indicates that she was also known for making and dyeing linen, hence the red cloth on her roof. It stands to reason that colored fibers would have been hung out to dry from her roof in the past.

Rahab's house was suitably placed on top of the well-fortified Jericho wall, making it conspicuous to wayfarers and others. On the other hand, its situation also allowed Rahab to survey the city below and be able to see the two Israelite spies slink in the gates before they arrived at her house. At first no one would have paid attention to two men heading toward a harlot's home on the less desirable side of town, but after a second glance, one of the king's servants may have noticed that they were dressed like Hebrews and alerted the palace about their presence inside the city. The king immediately sent a message to Rahab ordering her to turn over the spies to him, but she ignored his directive. She lied to the king's messengers, telling them that the men had left unnoticed in the darkness at the shutting of the gates. Her story convinced the messengers to pursue the spies without success. The messengers believed her because they had searched her house from top to bottom, even ascending to the roof where the spies were carefully hidden under her flax. While the messengers were out searching for the spies, Rahab let down them down the wall by a scarlet cloth that she had bound from her window. It seemed that she was familiar with the area around the city because she advised the spies to lodge in the mountains for three days until the pursuers returned and then continue on their journey back to their camp (Joshua 2:16). The spies did as she told them, and they returned safely to where the Israelites were camped.

To say that Rahab was courageous is an understatement because what she did was extraordinary. To the natural mind, she voluntarily entered into a foolish proposition and risked her and her family's lives for the sake of the enemy. Regardless of whether her way of life was fair or foul, it must be admitted that she was unusually perspicacious and skilled in business negotiations, skills she used effectively to secure the preservation of her family. She had more to gain by preserving her status as a loyal citizen of Jericho and trusting in the security of its visible fortifications than in helping the Israelites, who depended on the might of an invisible God to bring down the almost impregnable walls of Jericho.

The ragtag army of the nomadic, fledgling nation of Israel was no match for the sedentary people of Jericho who had time to develop weapons that would give them an edge in war over the Israelites, regardless of the latter's past victories against two Amorite territories east of Jordan.[10] Jericho was prepared for any war, even if its only preparation was the wall. Moses, before his death, warned the children of Israel in Deuteronomy 9:1 that the peoples they were going to dispossess when they crossed the River Jordan were occupants of well-fortified cities and

---

[10.] Numbers 21: Victory over Og and Sihon

mightier than they were. Therefore, Rahab made a calculated decision to believe God and sided with the Israelites against her own people although knowing that they were woefully ill-equipped for war. Her faith moved her to perform a noble deed that saved the lives of God's people because nothing in the scriptures tells us that the spies bribed or coerced her to assist them in their conquest of Jericho.

Dispensations of promise and grace

God has revealed Himself to humanity from the beginning of time and from generation to generation. He has not hidden who He is and what His purpose is for those on earth. In order to pinpoint the work and display of God's power on earth, theologians have come up with paradigms to specify when various aspects of God's interaction with humans have been most prominent, which they term "dispensations." As a disclaimer, God's intervention in the lives of people transcend time and space, although Bible scholars have agreed that there are seven dispensations during which God has revealed or is still revealing Himself and His purpose to us. However, only two will be mentioned here—the dispensation of promise and the dispensation of grace— because they play out in the lives of Rahab and the children of Israel.

The dispensation of promise was given first to Abraham, who heard the voice of God and obeyed Him. Because of his obedience, God promised to bless Abraham, provide an heir from him and Sarah, make his descendants prosperous, bless all the nations of the earth vicariously through the seed of Abraham who is Jesus Christ, decree the act of circumcision as a reminder of the covenant, and bless those who bless the children of Israel and curse those who curse them. The promise was also revisited with Isaac and Jacob.

During the time of Abraham, his people were serving idols and living carnally. If they heard the voice of God, many did not listen nor obey.

Nevertheless, one man did and received a promise that God has fulfilled and continues to fulfill. Rahab, when she acquired knowledge of the true God and her understanding was opened, also accepted the truth and did not reject the revelation as some did and some still do:

> because what may be known of God is manifest in them, for God has shown it to them. For since the creation of the world His invisible attributes are clearly seen, being understood by the things that are made, even His eternal power and Godhead, so that they are without excuse, because, although they knew God, they did not glorify Him as God, nor were thankful, but became futile in their thoughts, and their foolish hearts were darkened. (Rom. 1:19–21 NKJV)

The dispensation of promise was given specifically to the Jews, but the God of wisdom left room so other peoples of the earth could benefit. Jesus came in the flesh from Jewish heritage, but He was the way of escape for all humanity. One of the benefits of this dispensation was that God promised to bless others who blessed Israel. Rahab may not have known or understood all that God had promised, but she knew enough to purpose in her heart to bless Israel, and it was counted as great faith. It is apparent that she had converted to Judaism before she met the spies since she initiated the act of hiding them and lying to the king's messengers about their whereabouts.

God tried the heart of Rahab and knew there was virtue there, obscured by the harshness of the life she led. Despite the fact that she had resorted to lying, He still blessed her for her act of faith and not for the means that she used. Rahab was able to say with certainty that the Lord of the spies was God both in heaven and on earth and that she knew that He had given the land of Jericho to the Israelites. How could this harlot woman, a Gentile, be so sure that Israel would be victorious had not God ploughed the ground of her heart? She may have shocked the two spies when they heard her words and realized the extent of her faith:

> I know that the Lord has given you this land and that a great fear of you has fallen on us, so that all who live in this country are melting in fear because of you. We have heard how the Lord dried up the water of the Red Sea for you when you came out of Egypt, and what you did to Sihon and Og, the two kings of the Amorites east of the Jordan, whom you completely destroyed. When we heard of it, our hearts melted in fear and everyone's courage failed because of you, for the Lord your God is God in heaven above and on the earth below. (Josh 2:8–11 NKJV)

In Matthew 16:13 (NKJV), Jesus asked his disciples, "Who do men say that I the Son of Man am?" They told him that some thought he was John the Baptist and others thought he was Elias or the prophets. Jesus continued to question them and asked them to tell Him who they thought He was. Simon Peter replied, "Thou art the Christ, the Son of the living God" (v.16). Jesus responded, "Blessed art thou, Simon Barjona: for flesh and blood hath not revealed it unto thee, but my Father which is in heaven" (v.18). When Jesus asked that question, the eyes of the disciples had not yet been fully opened concerning the deity of Jesus. In order to grasp who Christ truly was, it had to be revealed by the Holy Ghost. Rahab was not a dumb woman by a long shot as shown in her negotiation with the spies and the well-thought-out manner in which she hid them when the king's messengers arrived. Nevertheless, she lacked the spiritual acuity to discern that nothing exists outside of God and that His power encompasses heaven and earth. In the same manner that Simon Peter discerned that Jesus was the Son of God by the Holy Spirit, Rahab also received her knowledge not by flesh or blood, but by God's own anointing.

She had never seen the parting of the Red Sea and walked across its bed on dry ground, gazed at the pillar of cloud by day and the pillar of fire by night, heard the awesome voice of God as he uttered the Ten Commandments from the smoking mountain of Mt. Sinai, or tasted the honey-like manna from the sky. Yet this heathen woman expressed unwavering faith in their God. Her belief in the righteousness of their God was so strong that she made them swear by His name to save her family because she was convinced that if held accountable by the Almighty God, they would not renege on their word:

> Now then, please swear to me by the Lord that you will show kindness to my family, because I have shown kindness to you. Give me a sure sign that you will spare the lives of my father and mother, my brothers and sisters, and all who belong to them— and that you will save us from death. (Josh. 2:12–13 NKJV)

Such deep affinity for her family seemed so incongruous in a harlot, but she was not a regular harlot. She displayed more faith in Yahweh without seeing His mighty miracles than many of the spies' predecessors who witnessed His phenomenal acts but were barred from entering the Promised Land because of their unbelief! Had not God chosen her to save her enemies even if most Israelites would think her not worthy to come into their camp, being a Gentile and, even worse, a prostitute?[11] However, they dared not challenge the sovereign God but submit to His will for:

> What if God, wanting to show His wrath and to make His power known, endured with much longsuffering the vessels of wrath prepared for destruction, and that He might make known the riches of His glory on the vessels of mercy, which He had prepared beforehand for glory, even us whom He called, not of the Jews only, but also of the Gentiles? (Rom. 9:22–24 NKJV)

[11.] See Numbers 5:2.

The Canaanite peoples, including the inhabitants of Jericho, indulged in idolatry and excesses of every conceivable form of immorality—licentiousness, sodomy, bestiality, child prostitution, and sacrifice—for an inordinately long time and had defiled the land. God was weary of their depravity, but He told Moses that He would not destroy them until their abominations had become too full. At the time He saw fit, God sent the Israelites to rid the land of the peoples who contaminated it and then occupy it. Yet, in that milieu of spiritual degradation, God was still looking for one to show His mercy and found Rahab.

It has always been the plan of God to reconcile humanity back to Him, even after his fall in the garden of Eden. Although He did not fully execute His plan until He sent Jesus to earth to die for humankind, He has always shown acts of grace toward His creation. The completion of humanity's reconciliation with God through Christ is the dispensation of grace, of which we are recipients. The premise of this dispensation is unmerited favor. To sum it all up as the writer states in Romans 5:8 (NKJV), "But God demonstrates His own love toward us, in that while we were still sinners, Christ died for us."

Rahab represents the grace that God has shown to humankind all through the ages. She received unmerited favor from God and in turn showed favor to her relatives. It was risky for Rahab to include her family in her "scheme" because someone could have leaked the information to the authorities, and she and other family members would have been killed for treason; spies within Jericho could have noticed the unusual gathering of all her relatives in her home and did further investigation; the extremely long red cloth in her window could have drawn the attention of a curious person even if they were used to seeing fabric hung there because of her work with the textile industry; and the worst scenario, the spies could have reneged on their word to her after returning to the Israelite camp. The last reason given here is plausible because Rahab confessed that the Jews completely destroyed the cities that they conquered: they did not leave man or beast alive. Her only hope was the Israelite God who showed Himself as a God of all peoples.

They call me a *harlot*, but ...

Things that are out of place with their surroundings, behaviors that do not conform to the norm, or anything that goes against the grain trigger our attention. Our focus on what is different is an expression of a built-in mechanism alerting us that there is a potential threat to or change in the status quo and helping us to adjust to the difference. However, difference is not always negative.

Rahab was a woman of contradictions. The biographical information about her in the Bible is sparse, but what we do know affords us a window into her life and helps us to draw some conclusions about who she was. She was a known innkeeper, prostitute, and maker of linen cloth. Her religion was polytheism, but she converted to Judaism. She was quick thinking, faithful, loyal, and courageous. We are introduced to her when Joshua sends two men to spy on the city of Jericho and they enter "an harlot's house, named Rahab" (Josh. 2). It appears from the use of the indefinite article *an* that there may have been other harlots in that city, but the spies decided to come to her lodging. In two of three books of the New Testament where she is mentioned (Heb. 11:31 and James 2:25), the definite article *the* is used to describe her. She is accorded the title of "the harlot Rahab" or "Rahab the harlot."

The differences between a *harlot named Rahab* and *Rahab the harlot* are more than grammatical. The term *harlot* carries its own connotations. For such a pejorative term to be permanently paired with one's given birth name appears to be an insult, especially when one has relinquished the lifestyle that goes with the term. It seems paradoxical to a postmodern reader that the writers of the books of Hebrews and James still attach the title of "the harlot" to Rahab's name while lauding her for her unmatched faith and works. Should a reader be skeptical of the writers' intent to honor Rahab or to conclude that the goal is to emphasize her spotty past? The answer to both questions is yes. The answer seems illogical, yet one is inclined to believe that the appearance of the title is intentional—like the omission of Bathsheba's given name in Matthew's genealogy of Christ, where she is referred to as *her that had been the wife of Urias* (Matt.1: 6). Having answered those questions, another question arises: Why?

The irony of the answer is to grasp the fact that such demeaning nomenclature attached to her birth name is not without merit, as will be subsequently explained. From experience, one tends to believe that people with titles are a cut above the rest: they are of noble birth, have accomplished feats, and have unusual abilities. Their titles tell who they are. For example, one is used to common names like Alexander the Great, John the Baptist, and Joan of Arc. If Rahab's name is indicative of the usual manner for conferring titles, the term harlot should have been removed since it does not reflect the lifestyle change that occurred in her after she converted to Judaism. Moreover, she became the wife of Salmon, believed to be one of the spies whom she hid in her house in Jericho (Matt. 1:5); therefore, her marriage to him should have removed any tarnish from her name.

It is interesting to note though that when Rahab's name appears with Salmon's in the same genealogy, the term harlot is omitted. Her given name also appears here as Rachab and not Rahab (1:5). Because there is a difference in the names, some scholars posit that Rahab the harlot is not same woman whose name appears in Matthew 1:5 and that she was not married to Salmon of the tribe of Judah.

However, it is not unusual to encounter slight differences in the spelling of a person's name in the Bible. For example, Bathsheba's name appears as Bathshua in 1 Chronicles 3:5. Therefore, the incredulity of some, regarding Salmon's marriage with Rahab, may stem from a reluctance to accept that a Canaanite harlot could be included in the ancestry of

King David and our Lord Jesus Christ. It is a fact that Rahab the harlot was accepted into and became a part of the Jewish nation (Josh. 6:25), so it is plausible that she could have been married to a grateful spy. God's thoughts are still higher than our thoughts, and his ways are different from ours. His words tell us in 1 Corinthians 1:27 (NKJV), "But God has chosen the foolish things of the world to put to shame the wise, and God has chosen the weak things of the world to put to shame the things which are mighty" in order to show us that He is sovereign.

Why Rahab?

So why then has the title stuck to his day, that even preachers in the twenty-first century cannot mention her without reference to her harlotry? The response to the question, although it indirectly takes into account that Rahab once engaged in harlotry, is not focused on her but rather on the far-reaching effect of God's dispensation of grace. In light of this understanding, the title is not a mark of offense; rather it is a term of endearment, a lasting emblem of honor to the faith of a Gentile woman and a testament to God's power in the lives of all peoples on the earth. The attachment of "harlot" to her name increases our admiration for her and gives us an appreciation for her remarkable transformation.

That God would use a vessel of dishonor and mold it into a vessel of honor, fit to be one of the matriarchal ancestors of His Holy Son, is beyond human understanding. It still baffles many that she is still remembered kindly and held in high esteem in both Jewish and Christian faiths. However, our fascination with her may be explained in one thing that moves the heart of God: faith. God is not impressed with our righteousness, nor is He moved by our needs as He is touched by our faith. How do we know?

Let's go back to instances when Jesus speaks about faith in the New Testament, especially His encounter with the centurion (Matt. 8:10) and His meeting with the Syrophoenician woman (Matt 15:21–28).

The centurion, recognizing the power and authority of Jesus, sent a subordinate to beg Him to heal his dying servant. However, while Jesus was on His way to fulfill the request, the centurion stopped Him and asked Him only to speak the word because as a Gentile he was not worthy enough to allow Jesus to enter his house. Jesus marveled at his humility and faith and exclaimed to the bystanders, "I say to you, I have not found such great faith, not even in Israel!" And those who were sent, returning to the house, found the servant well who had been sick (Luke 7:9–10 NKJV). The centurion did not deliberately plan to impress Jesus, but he did because he had faith. Likewise, the Syrophoenician woman moved Jesus's heart by her perseverance. She asked Jesus to heal her daughter, and Jesus objected. However, each objection that Jesus gave was followed by the woman's plea for the healing of her daughter. Jesus acquiesced and said to her, "Woman, you have great faith! Your request is granted," and her daughter was healed at that moment (Matt. 15:28 NKJV). On both occasions Jesus was very pleased with their actions, for without faith it is impossible to please God.

A memorial

On the eve of the crucifixion of Rahab's most illustrious descendant, Jesus Christ was invited to the home of Simon, the leper. A woman, believed to be a prostitute, heard that He would be present and decided to attend. When she arrived, she threw herself down at Jesus's feet and wept. She then took and broke the alabaster jar that she had brought with her and poured its content on His body and anointed His feet, kissing and wiping them with her hair (Luke 7:36–48). As the woman's hands gently rubbed the feet of Jesus while tears fell from her face, she ignited the anger of some onlookers, including Judas Iscariot who would later betray Jesus for thirty pieces of silver. The writers of Matthew, Mark, and John agree that the perfume she had used to perform this honorific act was very expensive, costing more than three hundred denarii, more than a year's wages during that time (Mark 14:3–9). This woman had done this act out of a sense of gratitude and love for Christ without being aware of the significance of her action while many of those who were close to Him missed the opportunity to minister to Him, including the host who invited Him to dinner. Jesus took note of the woman's gift of love and sacrifice and He said to the upset onlookers:

> For in pouring this fragrant oil on My body, she did it for My burial. Assuredly, I say to you, wherever this gospel is preached in the whole world, what this woman has done will also be told as a memorial to her. (Mark 14:8–9, Matt. 26:6–13 NKJV)

The story of this woman is mentioned here because she shares some similarities to Rahab. Both women were of disreputable character, but they both had a revelation about the identity of the true God. Neither of these women allowed fear, their past, nor the opinion of others to prevent them from seeking God's mercy and accepting His grace. They both, after receiving their revelation, purposed in their hearts and did acts to the glory and honor of God. Wherever their acts are mentioned, they serve as a memorial to their faith.

The scarlet thread

It is easy to overlook the fact that Rahab was an industrious woman because her involvement in prostitution has clouded this important facet of her personality. The scarlet thread, with which Rahab let down the spies, was not conjured out of space. It was there because this woman engaged in meaningful activity, and she took a natural fiber that she treated and carefully processed and made it into a less-refined linen than the factory-woven type we have today. The word *thread* is used in the Bible, but it is not the fragile thread normally used for sewing. Obviously, it would not have supported the weight of two strong men or been long enough to extend to or near to the base of the wall. It was apparently a rope made from fibers that Rahab had woven from flax and dyed red. It took several pieces of fabric or large numbers of fibers twisted and knotted together to make the rope sturdy and long enough to support the spies as they descended the wall. That the rope was scarlet and readily available appears to be coincidental. But how many instances in the scriptures has one seen how mundane things take on divine significance when one begins to understand that God works in various situations to bring about His desired end.

Rahab, in her desire to ensure that her kindness to the spies would be reciprocated in securing her safety and the safety of her relatives, asked that the spies not only swear to her by their God but also give her a sure token:

> Now therefore, I pray you, swear unto me by the Lord, since I have shewed you kindness, that ye will also shew kindness unto my father's house, and give me a true token. (Josh. 2:12 KJV)

She had no doubt that the Israelites would overthrow Jericho because she strongly stated that she believed in the awesome power of God in heaven and on earth (v.11). She also trusted that the spies would keep their word (v.14) because of their great fear of their God. However, she was aware that humans could forget. Therefore, she asked for tangible or visible proof from the spies that would remind her and them of the oath they had sworn so they would fulfill it. And what was more appropriate than the scarlet thread? The spies realized that since they were already familiar with it because Rahab had used it to let them down, and its color was easily seen, it would serve as the best thing to remind them of their oath to her:

> So the men said to her: "We will be blameless of this oath of yours which you have made us swear, unless, when we come into the land, you bind this line of scarlet cord in the window through which you let us down, and unless you bring your father, your mother, your brothers, and all your father's household to your own home. So it shall be that whoever goes outside the doors of your house into the street, his blood shall

be on his own head, and we will be guiltless. And whoever is with you in the house, his blood shall be on our head if a hand is laid on him. And if you tell this business of ours, then we will be free from your oath which you made us swear." Then she said, "According to your words, so be it." And she sent them away, and they departed. And she bound the scarlet cord in the window. (Josh 2:17–21 NKJV)

It may be that other than serving its purpose as a reminder of the oath they had sworn to Rahab, the scarlet thread hanging from her window held no other significance. However, during the three days hiding in the mountains, the spies may have reflected on the startling parallel between the scarlet thread and the blood sprinkled on the doorposts and on the lintels of the Hebrew houses the night before their ancestors left Egypt.

Exodus 12 tells the mighty manifestation of God's display of power on behalf of the children of Israel and His wrath on Pharaoh and Egypt. Despite the plagues God had brought on Egypt, Pharaoh's heart remained hardened and he refused to liberate the children of Israel. He and all parents of Egypt lost their firstborn sons and beasts the night before the children of Israel left Egypt because of his stubbornness. The children of Israel were spared this disaster because God commanded Moses to warn every Jewish household to take the blood of a young male lamb and plaster it on the doorposts and lintels of their houses as a sign. At midnight, when the Lord passed through Egypt and saw the blood on the doorposts and lintels, He spared them:

> For I will pass through the land of Egypt on that night, and will strike all the firstborn in the land of Egypt, both man and beast; and against all the gods of Egypt I will execute judgment: I am the Lord. Now the blood shall be a sign for you on the houses where you are. And when I see the blood, I will pass over you; and the plague shall not be on you to destroy you when I strike the land of Egypt. (v. 13 NKJV)

To the spies, the scarlet thread was a reminder of the blood of the Passover lamb painted on the doorposts of the Israelites in Egypt and a symbol to Rahab and her relatives that the God of Israel was a faithful God who shows mercy to all those who accept Him as Lord of their lives. That thread, drenched by the dust from the crumbled wall of Jericho, marked the precarious spot where Rahab's house still stood when everything else around it tottered to the ground. Amid the rubble and dead bodies of men and beasts, the spies brought her to safety with her relatives. How amazing that the great wall had completely collapsed, except where this harlot's house stood as a testament to all that in God all things consist—living and non-living!

Exhaustive archaeological work done during the 1950s and later revealed that the city wall of Jericho had caved in on itself and that a remnant of its northern part had remained intact. Bryant G. Wood notes in the article "The Walls of Jericho" (2008) that Katherine Kenyon, a highly acclaimed archaeologist, showed in the findings from her excavation of the city of Jericho between 1952 and1958 that a portion of a mud brick wall was still standing on the north end of the city. Her discovery, he states, was also supported by a German archaeological team that carried out excavations during the earlier part of the twentieth century. Today, the archaeological sites in and around the city of Jericho are some of the most visited Bible places because of one woman's faith and the invincible power of God.

Epilogue

The Scarlet Thread and the Blood

What does the "Star Spangled Banner" have in common with the scarlet thread in a harlot's window? Nothing, and yet something. Francis Scott Key, a lawyer and beloved writer of the American anthem, wrote this song after noticing the battle-weary flag waving defiantly in the aftermath of the Battle of Baltimore, part of the ongoing War of 1812.

Earlier Francis had gone to negotiate with the British to release a friend and some others who were held as prisoners on their ship. He gained their release, but only to be kept as hostages on their own ship under the watchful eyes of their captors who felt that, if fully released, they would alert the American military about the planned British attack on Fort McHenry. The British were fully prepared for war, and it appeared that the Americans were no match for them. Key and his colleagues braced themselves for an immediate victory for the British. He was convinced that he would see the proud Union Jack blowing in the early morning breeze and not the American flag. Imagine his surprise when he saw the star-spangled American banner flying above the fort.

Eons of years ago, a scarlet thread hung in a window as a sign of one woman's faith and a witness to the judgment and grace of God. After waiting many days, days that seemed like an eternity, Rahab and her family were literally able to breathe a sigh of relief as the two spies returned. True to their word and their God, they looked for the thread and followed it. Her family members, like the Americans, were imprisoned in their own space, except that with the Americans, imprisonment was involuntary, while with Rahab it was self-imposed for her and her family's protection. Both parties could have left their shelter (ship or house) at their own peril, but they were forced to remain where they were because they were potentially in danger from their allies and enemies alike during the frenzy of war. Neither Rahab nor the Americans knew what their fate would be, but both relied on a visible sign to bolster their spirits as they waited: for the Americans, a star spangled banner; for Rahab, a scarlet rope. Fortunately, the story bode well for both camps.

In the same manner that the stories ended well for Rahab and the Americans, the story of the believer in Christ will end well too. We have the cross to remind us that the work of redemption has been completed. Christ cried out on the cross after His blood was shed for the sins of all humankind, "It is finished!" The cross is the emblem of Christ's blood that is still able to save sinners as it continues its interminable flow from heaven to earth. From the moment God blew His breath into man and He became a "living soul," a blood connection was made because life is in the blood. When Adam sinned, a juncture was made in the line that allowed impurities to build up on humanity's end. Since there had to be a blood sacrifice for the absolution of a person's sin, God graciously allowed the priests temporary redemption by sacrificing animals on behalf of Israel. However, when the time was fully come, Christ offered a perfect sacrifice, once and for all, with His own blood. All other blood that was shed before Him was an imitation of His blood and could not satisfy the requirements for redemption.

This scarlet thread in Rahab's window represented the blood of Christ that was shed on the cross—a shadow of things to come. After Adam and Eve sinned in the garden, God clothed them in animal skins because they had lost their innocence and become aware of their nakedness. In essence, God performed the first blood sacrifice not only to provide skins to cover their physical bodies but also to cover their sins. The first sin of disobedience was the beginning of the slippery slope that would plunge them and their offspring into the spiraling abyss of sin and would require repeated sacrifices for them to have fellowship with God. However, animal blood lacked the efficacy to completely cover the sins of humankind once and for all. Therefore, God prepared a sure and pure sacrifice that would "not [be] with the blood of goats and calves, but with His own blood [He would enter] the Most Holy Place once for all, having obtained eternal redemption" (Heb. 9:12).

The raison d'être for Christ's incarnation is for the execution of divine law that states there is no remission of sin without the shedding of blood (Heb. 9:2). However, it was not the law that moved Him to come to earth and die, but it was His love for His creation that stirred Him to act on our behalf. Love prompted Him to offer grace to those who bore His image, howbeit a very tarnished one of Him. When God made man, He said, "Let us make man in our image, after our likeness" (Gen. 1:26), and equipped him with all that he needed for this and the eternal world. He did it by giving man the blood of life; with blood, man is able to replicate himself because in it he carries the seed for subsequent generations. Blood is the connection between the natural man and woman and Christ, and in order to maintain the link, we must abide in Him "for in Him we live, and move, and have our being" (Acts 17:28).

Before He came to earth as a man, Jesus showed His love to His ancestors. The first were Adam and Eve because He did not destroy them, but He became their way of escape from eternal death. He expressed His love toward Abraham and Sarah, Isaac and Rebekah, Jacob and Leah, Judah and Tamar, Rahab and Obed, Boaz and Ruth, David and Bathsheba, and Joseph and Mary, placing them in His human ancestry with all their human failings. They did not all commit vile sins, but all carried the Adamic blood and all were in need of a Savior whether they were living or dead.

References

Fletcher, Elizabeth. 2006. "Jericho Bible Archaeology." www.bible archaeology.info/bible_city_jericho.htm (accessed June 2, 2016).

Harrison, Roland Kenneth. 1969. *Introduction to the Old Testament with a Comprehensive Review of Old Testament Studies and a Special Supplement on Apocrypha.* 1st ed. Grand Rapids MI: William B. Eerdmans Publishing Company.

Leggett, Donald A. 1974. *The Levirate and Goel Institutions in The Old Testament.* Cherry Hill, NJ: Mack Publishing Company. https://faculty.gordon.edu/hu/bi/ted_hildebrandt/otesources/08-ruth/texts/books/leggett-goelruth/leggett-goelruth.pdf (accessed Jan. 30, 2016).

Lineberry, Cate. 2007. "The Story Behind the Star Spangled Banner." *Smithsonian* magazine, March 1. http://www.smithsonianmag.org (accessed May 31, 2016).

"What Are the Seven Dispensations" *Got Questions?org.* (accessed May 4, 2016).

Wood, Bryant G. 2008. "Walls of Jericho." Associates for Biblical Research, June 9. http://www.biblearchaeology.org/post/2008/06/09/The-Walls-of-Jericho.aspx (accessed May 4, 2016).

Printed in the United States
By Bookmasters